OTHER BOOKS BY ELIZABETH MCCORMICK

CAN Leadership

From the Soar 2 Success Tip Series

Soar 2 Success as a Speaker

Soar 2 Success: It's Not Stalking; It's Follow-Up

Soar 2 Success as an Entrepreneur

Soar 2 Success When Exhibiting at Events

Soar 2 Success in Network Marketing

Soar 2 Success in Network Marketing Leadership

Soar 2 Success in Direct Sales

Soar 2 Success in Direct Sales Leadership

**Meet Elizabeth online and receive free training at
www.Soar2Success.com**

THE P.I.L.O.T. METHOD

THE 5 ELEMENTAL TRUTHS TO LEADING YOURSELF IN LIFE!

ELIZABETH McCORMICK

NEXT CENTURY
PUBLISHING

Published by Next Century Publishing
NextCenturyPublishing.com

Printed in the United States of America

ISBN: 9781629030081

Dedicated to my Keeper Husband

Keith

Because you...

Believe in my Potential
Support my Implementation
Encourage my Leadership
Remind me to Optimize
Stand next to me in Tenacity

I'm so thankful you stopped
looking, so you could find me.

A NOTE FROM THE AUTHOR

When I was serving in the U.S. Army, my mom would show pictures of me with the helicopter to everyone she knew. It was embarrassing to me, because it wasn't a big deal. Everyone I worked with was a Pilot too.

It wasn't until I got out of the military and was into a civilian job and involved in my community in Texas, that I realized being a Pilot was special. And now as a full time professional motivational and leadership speaker, I bring those stories to audiences and relate them to life and business.

What I learned is that Pilots ARE different. We think differently due to our training and living on the brink of life and death at the whim of a machine. My goal with this book is to share that thinking with you, to shift your perspective, so that you can lead yourself in life. Because we have to lead ourselves before we can lead others.

Some of the names have been changed. And the experiences I went through are how I remember them, and it's been a few years. If there are mistakes in this book, please know they are not intentional, and my stories are based purely on my memory and the resources that are still available to me.

It's an honor to share these elemental, basic truths with you and it is my hope that you will benefit from this book and Soar 2 Success!

Wishing you great success!
SOAR!

Elizabeth McCormick

ACKNOWLEDGMENTS

Thank you to everyone who made this book possible:

First, always first, my family, Keith, Adara, and Luke, for putting up with my late nights and deadlines and still loving me as much as I love you!
You are my heart.

Carla Spurgeon, my personal assistant.
Without her, things would not get done.

My book team,
Christine Whitmarsh and Feisty Michelle at Christine, Ink., for editing and for cracking the whip to keep me on track to meet the deadline.
You make me sound great!

Chris Mendoza for the cover design, illustrations, and formatting.
You make me look great!

And the pilots for contributing their stories to make this book even better:

Doug Petersen
Kimberly Olson
Buck Burney
Dan Bornarth
Carol (last name withheld upon request)
Tom Martinelli
Dale Edelmann

CONTENTS

Potential

The P.I.L.O.T. Method

CHAPTER 1

POTENTIAL

I had no idea how dramatically my life was about to change.

I was an unemployed military wife, stationed at Fort Polk, Louisiana. Make that we were stationed in Fort Polk, Louisiana. I had learned quickly that, as a military wife, everything was a collective we. "We" were in the field. "We" were deploying. "We" were reassigned. Being a military wife is more than a marital status; it's a way of life.

The ink was barely dry on my college diploma when I packed up everything I owned from my soon-to-be (and should-have-already-been) condemned apartment, shoved all I could into my bright blue Pontiac Sunbird, and headed south from Michigan to Louisiana to be with my military husband. Newly wed in December and now newly graduated, I was excited for what the future would hold.

I wasn't a stranger to the South. For more than ten years, I had spent summers with my father in Texas. It was part of the life of the child of divorced parents with jobs in different states. I spent school years in Michigan living with my mom and summers in Texas

visiting my dad. So the heat wasn't a surprise. The lack of available jobs, however, came as a stark shock.

I had worked since the age of thirteen. My first job was working for my dad's construction company. I was his daughter, but that didn't mean I received special treatment. From day one, I was bleaching mold off walls or painting racks in warehouses or working the equipment on assembly lines—anything my young hands could handle.

Growing up in a construction family wasn't, "You can't do that." It was, "*Can* you do that?" It wasn't a gender issue; it was all about skill and strength.

In retrospect, I see that my father was a man of quiet competence. He didn't discourage the development of potential in either me or my siblings.

> ### *Potential (noun): a latent excellence or ability that may or may not be developed.*

Now, I have to admit I had to look up latent. It means "present but not visible," but I want to paraphrase that original definition:

> ### *Potential (noun): a present but not visible excellence or ability that may or may not be developed.*

Notice the definition of *potential* does not specify who has it. Potential is always present. We all have it within us.

My father encouraged development of the potential in me through his words and by his actions. When he saw the

18

construction industry and his company's work dwindling during the cold, northern winter months, he started taking business classes at the local college at night.

Both of my parents went back to school as non-traditional students. First, my mom went to college while working full-time at K-Mart during the day. She went to night school, and when she wasn't in class or at work, she would study, sometimes all night long. After my mom graduated, it was my dad's turn. He immediately enrolled in school and mimicked my mom's ambitious study schedule while working in a men's clothing store during the day.

They were developing their potential! The influence they had on me during my impressionable preteen years left an indelible mark. They didn't give up. They didn't succumb to their circumstances. They didn't say, "We're in Michigan. The economy is bad. The weather is bad. Let's go on welfare." They MADE their circumstances BETTER. They made themselves better. It inspired me, and it formed me into a person who was willing to work hard to succeed. They showed me that you don't have to settle for the circumstances you are in. You have a choice.

When you can't change your circumstances, focus on what you can change within you.

When I was at Fort Polk, I was frustrated and unfulfilled. I applied for what felt like a hundred different jobs. Month after month, application after application, I waited to hear something. But I didn't. My student loans were coming due, looming over my head, and I needed to come up with a way to make the payments.

19

I knew I had to make a change. There was more than frustration in me. There was restlessness inside, a quiet unrest that whispered:

"Do NOT *settle."*
"You are meant for more."

There was a yearning in me to find something I had yet to experience. I knew that there was more within me, but in my inexperience, I didn't know how to find it. The consciousness of your unknowing heightens your awareness of self and the need to learn.

Did I understand what that feeling was at the time?
No.
Did I approach my lack of satisfaction with the feeling that I was entitled to receive something more?
No.
Did I know what I needed to do?
Not a clue.

I only knew that if I wanted something different to happen in my life, I would need to act differently to MAKE it happen!

My circumstances in Fort Polk were limiting. I was a newlywed, and I wanted to stay with my husband. But I also wanted the satisfaction that came with work. Aside from the new Wal-Mart, there just wasn't much opportunity there.

Then one day, I got a call. A Pizza Pizza franchise wanted to hire me as an assistant manager trainee. Five years of college, a bachelor's degree in art with a minor in mathematics, and an

associate's degree in science, and the only job I could get was working at a pizza place? I took the job. I had to DO something productive, and at the time, it was the best option I had.

During this time, my grandfather was dying from a surgery complication. I remember sitting on the concrete curb in the apartment complex parking lot, hurting and crying because I couldn't go to my grandfather. I had to stay in Fort Polk because someone had to make the pizzas. We couldn't afford the trip anyway.

That experience was my first brush with the responsibilities of adulthood. In that moment, I learned the difference between *working for spending money and working for a living*.

I knew that working in a pizza place wasn't going to be enough. I knew that my quiet unrest would not go away. I knew something had to change. And I knew change wasn't going to just happen for me. I had to make it happen, starting by acknowledging my own potential and recognizing that there was MORE than this.

Remember:

Potential is a present but not visible excellence or ability that may or may not be developed.

You have potential! Every single one of us has potential. I guarantee that, wherever you are in your life, your career, your education, you have more in you.

Accept it.
Choose to believe it.

I had to DECIDE to choose to do something different. One thing is ABSOLUTELY certain: *Your potential will not be realized if you* DO *the* same things *you've already been doing*.

But before you actually change, you need to make a decision—one that requires you to be open to the possibilities around you.

The power to make that decision is something every single one of us has within. If you want something different to happen in your life, it is up to you to act differently and MAKE it happen!

CHAPTER 2

THE DECISION

As soon as I made the decision to make a change, even though I had no idea what that change was going to be, the weight of dissatisfaction lightened. Finally, I felt like I was on the right path. But the sense of urgency was still there.

Along with the urgency was confusion. You see, I am not an intuitive person by nature. Did I mention I had a minor in mathematics? Logic and planning were in my comfort zone.

I learned to step out of my comfort zone and try new things, and today, as a professional keynote speaker, I don't even know where my comfort zone is anymore! I've gotten comfortable with being uncomfortable, in a near-constant state of growth and development.

But back then, logic ruled. I would carefully research and plan all my steps, weighing the possibilities for failure and success. My method was to think through decisions and imagine the possible outcomes: worst case, best case, and everything in between.

The thought process behind the decision-making looks like this:

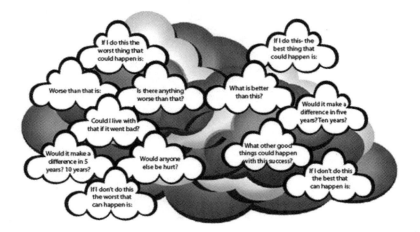

Even now, this is my thought process through every decision. Sometimes I write it out. Most of the time, it's in my head as I discard and prioritize possibilities and scenarios.

What I didn't know at the time was that pilots are trained in this process of anticipating every possible consequence. Typically, when there is an emergency in an aircraft, it's not just one emergency; it's a compound emergency.

In a delicate balance of flight, when one system goes out, another system is affected. Pilots prepare for these situations with simulator training, quizzing, and bookwork and by thinking through scenarios.

When that emergency happens for real, there won't be time to look it up in a book. There won't be time to hesitate. It must be

automatic muscle memory. Pilots know if this happens, then this happens, and then this action needs to be taken.

The outcome, crashing or not crashing, is dependent upon the ability to sort out those layers of emergencies, immediately evaluate the urgency, mentally organize the priorities, and DECIDE to implement emergency procedures—all while maintaining aircraft control, airspeed, altitude, course direction, and communication. With passengers, expensive airframes, and lives on the line, this becomes a critical skill.

In your life, your career, your calling, it's *your* life on the line. Maybe it is not life or death, but the QUALITY of your life is dependent on the QUALITY of the decisions you make.

There I was, not yet a pilot, mired in that decision-making process. I focused on what I knew—not what I *thought* but what I *knew*.

I made a list of what I knew to be true. I called this my "Know It All" list. I was making fun of myself because I knew there was so much I didn't know!

"Know it All"

- Knew change was coming and I was willing to be open to that change.

- I had a college degree.

- I was so far unable to get a local job other than in fast food.

- I wanted a job that allowed me to continue living with my husband.

- I could do anything but had no practical experience.

- I needed experience.

- I was physically fit and played college sports.

Armed with this "Know It All" knowledge, what could I do? What potential did I have within this knowledge? It gave me a starting point to look at my own circumstances differently.

26

I thought about this list. To think requires space and quiet. Turn off the TV, turn off the iPod, and turn off the computer. Turn off the distractions and the noise, and spend some quiet time thinking—just thinking.

For me, that time came in the middle of the night. I'd just gotten home from work, and I could still smell the yeasty dough and spices of the tomato sauce on my skin. It was 2:00 a.m., and aside from the hum of the refrigerator and the even breathing of Matt, my husband, the apartment was quiet.

Despite having worked on my feet for eight hours, I couldn't sleep. I lay in the inky blue darkness, looking at the shaved head of my husband, and thought and thought... *If my husband can be in the military, why can't I? Why CAN'T I? Could I? Physically, I could. I'd played college volleyball; it couldn't be harder than that, could it?* The questions came faster and faster, whirling through my head with a force that left me breathless. Could I handle the discipline? Could I withstand the conforming?

I started thinking through that decision-making process. *After training, Matt and I could be stationed at the same base. We'd have even more in common after sharing those experiences.* It hit me like a flash of lightning. THIS was a start.

And the unrest within me rested. I fell asleep.

The next morning, the doubts came streaming in. Who did I think I was? Did I have the physical strength to make this happen? Did I have the discipline—not my strong suit—to succeed? How would I fit in?

My logic kicked in and overrode the doubts. *I'll research it.* I thought of my husband's field ambulance unit at Fort Polk. I called his platoon leader, First Lieutenant Ashley, to see if she would join me for lunch.

Pulling my blue car into the parking lot outside the dirt-brown unit building, I realized I hadn't told my husband I was coming. I hadn't even discussed this with him first. I gnawed on my lower lip. *Should I ask him to come with us?*

Hesitation kept me in the car a minute longer. I needed a woman's point of view. I knew nothing about being a woman in the military. Was it even possible for me to do what I was thinking about doing?

I got out of the car and straightened my khaki pants and striped, button-up shirt. I was still in my pizza uniform. Ignoring the tomato sauce splatter stains, I walked into the dimly lit battalion's field ambulance bays. Ashley, a cute brunette with a fun, sassy attitude, was in the platoon leader's office she shared with the other leaders.

"Hey, Elizabeth!" she said and gave me a pat on the arm. Hugging was not allowed in uniform.

"Can we go for a drive for lunch?" I asked nervously, still looking around for my husband.

"Do you want anyone to join us? Matt's cleaning weapons in the armory today."

I shook my head and breathed a sigh of relief.

28

"Then let's go." She grabbed her Battle Dress Uniform (BDU) cap and we headed out to my car, which was parked in the visitor parking lot.

"You're being so secretive! What's this about?" Ashley asked as I put the key in the ignition.

"Do you like being in the Army?" I pulled out of the lot and headed toward the on-base Burger King.

"I do. There are lots of good things about being in the Army. I went ROTC in college, so they paid for school. Now I'm an officer." I heard her enthusiasm when she spoke.

"What's it like being a woman in the Army? That's what I really want to know, Ashley."

"Are you thinking about joining the Army?" She sounded shocked.

"I don't know. I know I'm not satisfied with this." I gestured toward my pizza manager uniform. "It's not enough. I didn't go to college for this. There's something more for me out there. I just don't know what that is."

"Honest truth?" She cocked her head at me and smiled. "It's hard. Most of the guys either don't want you here, hit on you because you are here, or don't take you seriously. We have to be better and smarter just to have a chance of being respected. It's not fair, but it's the truth."

29

I sat in silence, processing what she had told me and wondering if I could live with that. I knew I could. But then I said, "I can't do ROTC. I'm already out of college. What could I do if I joined the Army?" A shiver ran down my spine as I voiced the words for the first time.

We spent the rest of our lunch hour talking about Military Occupational Specialties—MOS—also known as your job. We talked about the different ways to get into the military as an officer. Since I had the college degree, I qualified to go in directly as an officer.

The decision was made. I could be an officer. But what job in the military? I was a twenty-three-year-old woman with multiple college degrees. What was the coolest job? With my limited experience and knowledge of the military, I didn't know the difference between a "good" job, a "bad" job," or a "cool" job.

More research. This was *my life, my future*. Wasn't I worth the research?

Back then, the Burger King was the only restaurant on base. I waited there, and every time an officer came in and sat down, I'd walk over and ask:

"If you had to do it over, what would you do differently?"
"If you could have any job, what would you want and why?"
"What is the coolest job in the Army?"

Over and over, with my notepad and pen in my hands, I heard:
"I'd be a helicopter pilot."
"If I had perfect eyesight, I'd fly."

"You could be a pilot!"

Helicopter pilot. Sounded like a cool job to me. *Why not? If I joined the Army, why couldn't I be a pilot?*

One day, I drove the long way to the pizza joint, down the flight line road. Before reaching the hangars and operations areas, I pulled my little car to the side of the road and stared at the helicopters lined up on their concrete pads. I stepped over the weeds in the ditch and stood in the knee-high grass along the chain-link security fence. I put my hand through the hot grey metal and studied the helicopters. *Could I do this?* That tingle of awareness ran through me again, and in a flash, I knew I could.

This was what I was meant to do.

The closest I'd come to flying was being one of the 200 passengers on an airliner. I knew nothing about it. I knew nothing about the process to get into flight school. Yet I knew with certainty I was going to fly. I saw myself in that olive green flight suit and climbing into that helicopter. It became very real.

All of this started with a decision; nothing can start without one. If you don't make the decision to be open to the opportunities around you, they will pass you by before you ever see them.

You are responsible for developing your own potential. All you have to do is believe.

31

CHAPTER 3

BELIEVE

I had the vision. I had the belief. I had no idea what to do with it. I had no idea how it was going to happen.

Here is where many of us make mistakes. We let "reality" or doubts get in the way of believing in our own potential. Or worse, we make it conditional: When I receive this promotion, I'll develop my potential.

Remember my "Know It All" list? I updated that list to reflect my new direction:

I knew I was going to join the Army.
I knew I was going to become an officer.
I knew I was going to FLY.

Even though I had never done it before, even though I had no idea how, I knew.

My job was to BELIEVE. Simple? Yes. Easy? No!

I reverted back to what I knew from my own experience. I researched. I went back to that flight line. I walked into the aviation unit and asked if I could talk to an officer.

A captain (I didn't know he was the company commander!) was willing to talk to me. I peppered him with questions while I took notes.

"If you could do anything differently, what would you do?" I asked.

He leaned toward me like he was going to tell me a secret and whispered, "I'd be a warrant officer!"

My first question was, "What's that?"

(See the inset box to the right for the explanation I received.)

Then I asked him, "Can you introduce me?" He led me to a different office where a small group of men were sitting around reading technical and operator manuals and studying flash cards.

The captain introduced me. "She has questions; help her out." Then he left.

> Difference between warrant officers and "real" officers in the Army:
>
> "Real" officers (as warrant officers refer to them) are the commissioned officers coming through the ROTC and OCS programs, ranking from lieutenant up to general. These officers are groomed to lead; their primary job is to command, and flight time can be secondary.
>
> Warrant officers were created for those jobs that require full-time skill, and their appointment is based on technical and tactical proficiency. The first warrant officers took care of the horses for the generals, a full-time job. Now it's a different kind of horsepower: helicopters.

34

Every eye in the room looked at me. I had my notepad and my list of questions, so I cleared my throat and shuffled my feet and said, "How do I become a warrant officer? I want to fly." The warrant officers relaxed with my question, invited me to sit, and shared with me.

I left that day with a clear understanding of the how. But it took a few days to persuade my husband to believe in me as much as I believed in me. And my parents thought I was crazy. It was so "unlike" me.

I was firm in my belief. I was going to be a warrant officer helicopter pilot. I said it over and over, out loud, believing it, relishing in it. After being held captive in the cold and dark of indecision, I was basking in the hot, yellow heat of the sun of knowing.

The next step in my journey was going to the recruiter to start the process. That August summer morning, I went to the recruiting station in Leesville, Louisiana, a small, narrow, cramped office in a strip mall not far from the new Wal-Mart.

Pulling open the glass door and stepping in, I had to admit I didn't look like a strong candidate. Outwardly there was nothing unique about me. But I had belief—belief in my own potential.

I walked into the recruitment office and Staff Sergeant Lewis stepped away from the sparse metal desk and greeted me.

"Hi!" he said with over-exuberance, his slick demeanor reminding me of a used car salesman. "We have openings for a cook today."

A cook? I was already miserable working in a pizza place. I squared my shoulders and thrust my chin out. "I'm here for the Warrant Officer Flight Training Program." The warrant officers on the flight line had given me the right terminology to say.

He laughed. Laughed! I felt small and insignificant in that moment. Doubts crept in. My inner voice fought those doubts. No, this is what you are meant to do! I believed in me. "I'm here for the Warrant Officer Flight Training Program," I repeated, stronger, louder, and firmer.

He stopped laughing. "You can't do that!"

"Why not?" was my immediate response, asked with pure curiosity.

"You need perfect eyesight."

"I have that."

"You need perfect physical condition." He raised an eyebrow in question.

"I have that."

"You need a college degree." He cockily stated. "I have three," I said.

"You need leadership experience." His voice rose to a higher pitch.

"I have that, too." Now I was really curious. What was standing in my way? What could it be?

Staff Sergeant Lewis stuttered and sputtered, "Because...because...uh...um..." and trailed off.

Again I asked, "Why not?"

"Well..." he answered sheepishly, "I don't know how to do the paperwork."

Imagine if, when I had first walked in, I had believed that recruiter more than I believed in myself. I might not have expanded my potential.

One of my two favorite quotes of all time is:

"Whether you think you can, or you think you can't —you're RIGHT."
~Henry Ford

Belief is the foundation to leading yourself and then others. Belief builds our confidence and allows us to handle situations that challenge us. You've probably already encountered people who don't believe in you. They are the negative nellies, the naysayers, the downers. Every time you have an idea, a belief or a vision that fires you up, these people splash cold water on your flames.

Me, too! You're not alone. We all face these challenges in our lives. It's how we react to that "feedback" that makes the impact.

What strategy can you use to prevent the negativity and doubters from affecting your destiny?

Negative thoughts, whether they come from us or from others, are just "feedback." They are no more right than positive beliefs. What matters is what we do with those negative thoughts, how we react to them.

Do we give those thoughts more space and weight in our thinking than the positive thoughts of what we hope to accomplish?

The negative thoughts do serve a purpose, and it's not necessarily to distract you from your goal. Those negative thoughts can be a warning sign to a potential roadblock or detour ahead. When you listen to those negative thoughts, write them down and use them to build strategies needed to overcome obstacles; they serve a useful purpose for you. Once you've done that then delete that thought. After you have wrung all the usefulness from that thinking, it doesn't serve you anymore. If that thought sticks around, it will become a distractor.

If you make the decision to handle a thought in that way—yes, you get to choose the thoughts that stay—that thinking advances you toward your goals.

By not making a choice to be aware and monitor your own beliefs, you are making the choice to give other people's beliefs value in your thinking. *You* make your thoughts work for you. Control *your* thinking.

CHAPTER 4

EXPECTATIONS

The last chapter in this section on Potential is about setting expectations. I expected to make it through flight school. It was not that "failure is not an option." It never occurred to me that I could fail. I didn't know how. I believed and expected that I could learn the way and make it happen, instead of waiting for it to happen.

It surprised me that I met obstacle after obstacle.

At the appointment on base at Fort Polk, the flight doctor, a barrel-chested officer in the later years of his career, looked at my paperwork. He glanced at me over his bi-focal glasses. "Little girl, don't you know flight school is hard?"

Overly polite, being careful with my words and tone, I responded, "Sir, I have an appointment. So no matter what you believe, let's just do this physical."

My next stop was the government facility in Shreveport, Louisiana—the MEPS (Military Entrance Processing Station). Here I would take my FAST (Flight Aptitude Skills Test). The older, senior,

noncommissioned officer administering the test said, "What makes you think you can do this? You're wasting your time."

I had a little more practice being tolerant this time. I looked at him and said, "Sergeant, I aced Calculus Four in college. I'm pretty sure I can handle a military standardized test." I smiled.

He "harrumphed" and slapped the test down in front of me.

I didn't believe it was hard. When you believe something is hard, it's usually hard. When you believe something is easy, it ends up being easy—or at least not as hard.

However, every step of the process there was an obstacle I had to overcome.

Just because there are bumps or detours in your path, that doesn't mean you aren't going to get there. I learned that there will not only be potholes in your road, but sometimes you will have to put the car in four-wheel drive and go around the road. The path you've chosen might not be available right now. Maybe more learning, more experience, more seasoning in life is needed. Timing is a tricky thing like that. Very rarely is your path to success a straight course.

When you believe in yourself *and* expect greater success, it's difficult to quit, even when the going gets tough.

There was one final step in building my application packet to Warrant Officer Flight Training before it went to the selection committee at the Pentagon. I had to drive from Fort Polk to the National Guard command in Baton Rouge where they were

conducting promotion board interviews. Typically, this is where an enlisted sergeant goes in dress uniform before a board of officers, answers questions, and shows his or her readiness for promotion.

I had to go before this same promotion review board to be evaluated for my suitability to be a warrant officer and an aviator. My stomach was in jitters all through the three-hour drive. Once there, I changed into a dress suit and put my long hair into a bun, as if I were already in service. My hands shook as I prepared myself in the ladies' room.

I looked at my image in the mirror and said:

"I've got this.
I am going to be a pilot.
I am articulate.
I am strong.
I am the best candidate.
I am smart."

When I went into the boardroom and faced the panel of officers reviewing me, I wasn't as nervous. I did have this. And as amazing as it sounds, they needed me to succeed, too. I was a strong candidate and would represent them well. Because of that, I received the highest marks the promotion board could give—top blocks all the way across, with comments like:

"Absolute 'Must Select.'"
"Would want her in my unit as top aviation warrant."
"Most impressive applicant I've seen."

It was the first sign of encouragement I had received, and with that, my packet was complete to go to the Pentagon. My packet carried the paper equivalent of my future: my flight physical, my testing scores, letters of recommendation from my professors and employers while in college, the application, the security clearance application, and the results of the promotion board. All I had to do now was wait.

My packet had gone in too late to be considered by the November Recruiting Command Selection Board. I had to wait close to a month for the December board to meet. I was still working at the pizza place, although now officially promoted to Manager in Training.

Three months earlier, when I was hired, I had told the owner that my sister was getting married in Texas over Thanksgiving weekend, and I was in the wedding. I would take the time off work unpaid, but I needed that long weekend. My expectation was that I would get that time off.

The week before the wedding, the District Manager who was training me sent out the schedule. Despite reminders, I was scheduled to work. At the age of twenty-three, I was still learning skills like being tactful. I called the District Manager and went on the attack.

The strong-willed District Manager attacked back. "Too bad; you're on the schedule!"

I walked off the job. In my state of anger, I felt justified; I had been promised this time off, but not by the District Manager. The owner had made that commitment to me. In a rage, I did

something I would not have done if I had been thinking rationally.

It's funny how things become so obvious afterwards. With the crystal clear clarity of hindsight, I knew I should have called the owner and communicated with him directly, reminding him of our hiring agreement. It should have been a calm and rational discussion, with me offering to create an alternate schedule with the staffing covered. I could have been part of the solution.

But I wasn't. I didn't handle it maturely. I didn't handle it correctly, and I burned that bridge unnecessarily. After walking off the job, I went to my sister's wedding and returned to Louisiana four days later. There were several messages on my home answering machine from the owner.

Even then, I should have called him back, and we probably would have been able to work something out. But at that point, I was embarrassed by my behavior. Although I expected to get the time off, I realized the owner also expected me to act like the manager he had hired me to be. And I hadn't met my end of those expectations.

Now I was unemployed for who knew how long, without a reference, and I was still waiting to receive word if I would be "picked up" by the next selection board. I had made a mistake I regretted.

Expectations are a two-way street. There are the expectations you have, and there are the expectations others have of you. We often forget that we are held to others' expectations, like those of the pizza franchise owner. Disappointment occurs when expectations aren't met, aren't communicated, or are unrealistic.

43

I've heard a lot of people say, "If I don't expect too much, I won't be disappointed."

That thinking creates a fine line. I believe that we should expect big things, even great things, of ourselves, and when it comes to others, we should clearly communicate our expectations to prevent disappointment.

I expected to be selected for Warrant Officer Flight Training. And at the December selection board meeting, I was.

IMPLEMENTATION

CHAPTER 5

IMPLEMENTATION TAKES DISCIPLINE

I made it. I remember getting the phone call from the recruiter. I wasn't excited because I expected it. I knew I was going to make it. Sergeant Lewis was very surprised though, almost shocked. At first, we didn't have a lot of details, and then the orders came through. I was to report to basic training in Fort Jackson, South Carolina, on March 15, just over two months away.

I was unemployed so I didn't have any excuses or distractions. I treated my pre-basic training days like a full-time job. I ran, I worked out, I went into my husband's unit and, with their permission, did physical fitness training with them. I learned some basic soldiering skills.

I had to get it done. I didn't want to go into basic training and then immediately after enter into Warrant Officer Candidate School (WOCS) with any kind of deficit. I figured I'd probably be okay in basic training. But in WOCS, I would be in class with seasoned, enlisted and noncommissioned officers, and there wouldn't be any second chances.

47

The time slid away. When you're so focused on something, the days on the calendar just spin away from you. It seemed like I blinked and it was time to go.

The night before my bus departure to Fort Jackson, my friend, Lieutenant Ashley, gave me the Army Officer Guide Book. "You're going to need this where you're going." On that long bus ride from Louisiana to South Carolina, I studied that book. I visualized the marching skills I had learned, and while I slept, I dreamt of flying helicopters.

The military is a harmony of "hurry up and wait." Nowhere, and I mean nowhere else, have I ever experienced that like I did while serving in the U.S. Forces.

In the beginning of basic training, the "reception" phase, we moved as a group, a platoon, to receive our clothing issue (taken out of our pay), waited in line to get our clothing, and continued waiting until everyone else was done. Then we moved back to the sleeping barracks.

Immunizations were given with a multi-needle power gun to give all the shots with one "stick." After seeing the needles tear the skin and cause blood to stream down the bicep of one soldier who flexed his muscle during the injection, word quickly whispered down the line: "Relax your arm during the shot!"

And the paperwork! No one likes paperwork like the military likes paperwork. Life insurance? No life insurance? Who would be the benefactor of your life insurance? Invest in a monthly payment to a college savings plan (the Montgomery GI Bill), or not? Most of the adults working their way through the line had just turned

eighteen-years old, and those were the first decisions they were making on their own. No guidance could be given. The decisions were theirs and theirs alone.

A recruiter hadn't told one female soldier that in order to continue into basic training, she would have to assign someone else as the legal guardian of her child. She would have to give away her parental rights while in training. Without signing that paperwork, she could not move on. She was stuck in the reception area until she made a decision. She not only had to decide whether to give up her rights, but with very little family, she had to determine to whom she could give those rights. I heard her crying that night. When it was time for the limited phone time we had, she was first in line. She didn't continue on with the rest of us. It was a time of difficult, grown-up decisions.

There was physical training in that pre-basic training mode. In order to continue on to basic training, females had to be able to do one push-up—One!—a "man's style" push-up, up on the toes, back perfectly straight, with the body moving in one continuous movement until the upper arms were parallel to the ground at a perfect ninety-degree angle between the elbow and the upper arm. After months of training, I could do eighteen.

What was incredible to me was that there were some females who could not do ONE. Not ONE! They all signed enlistment contracts with their recruiters. They knew they were going in. They even knew the date they were going in. But they didn't implement. They had to spend more time in reception getting physically fit, lifting soup cans at night to build muscle and stamina.

49

After about a week, the majority were deemed ready. We were ordered to load our gear into a duffel bag and get on "the bus." If you've served in the American Armed Forces, there are all kinds of stories of "the bus." It's a normal yellow school-style bus, but the stories are about the abrupt transition from an in-processing environment to a full-out disciplinary environment.

The bus transported us across base to our new unit for basic training and what would be our home for the next eight weeks.

As the bus slowed to a stop, the door opened, and our first drill sergeant stepped into the bus.

All drill sergeants wear a distinctive Smoky Bear style hat. It has brown felt with a stiff, wide brim to shade the eyes. That drill sergeant also sported mirrored sunglasses and looked mad as all get-out. The nervous tittering of forty-two females on the bus faded to tense silence.

Bellowing at the top of his lungs, the drill sergeant yelled, "You will get off this bus, carry your duffel bag on your back, and march up the stairs to the barracks. You are in A Company, 1st Platoon. You will find your bunk and empty your duffel on the bunk. You will stand at the position of attention." He stopped, looking at us.

"Well? What are you waiting for? *Go, go, go!*" We slung the duffel bags that had been on our laps during the bus ride over our shoulders, crowded off the bus, and scrambled for the stairs. The entire time Drill Sergeant Gills and his assistant Drill Sergeant Barnes were screaming at us: "Get up those stairs! GO! Why are

you moving so slowly?" It was intimidation at full force, and it worked.

We got to the top of the stairs. Forty-two bunks were lined up in four rows in the living barracks. There was pushing from behind as everyone rushed to get in. I walked up and down the rows, looking at the end of bunk after bunk for my name on tape. Mine was the closest to the drill sergeant's office. Great.

The shouting followed us into the barracks bay. I hurriedly unbuckled my duffle, dumped it on the bed, and stood at attention with my back straight, arms straight, eyes straight ahead, fingers curled with the thumb pressed against the index finger knuckle.

The drill sergeants, ours and several other visiting ones, walked through the bay, stopping at every bunk to sift through personal belongings. The message was clear: "You're only allowed to have what we want you to have." When Drill Sergeant Gills came to my bunk, he picked up that Army Officer Guide Book.

Loudly he said, "OOOOOOOHHHHHH, this one hasn't even made it through basic training, and she thinks she's an officer!" With his mirrored sunglasses still on, he stepped in front of me with the guidebook in his hand.

I was still so firm in the belief that that was what I was going to do and that, in my expectation, it was going to happen, that I smiled! (Go ahead and shake your head while you're reading this!) I said firmly, "Yes, I will be, Drill Sergeant." After all, I hadn't packed for basic training. I had packed for my entire journey. There was no doubt that I could finish basic training. I was focused on what I needed to do for WOCS.

"Did you see that?" He raised his voice even louder, hailing the other drill sergeants to stop their inspections and come to my bunk. "She smiled at me. She thinks she's going to be an officer, and she hasn't even finished basic training." He showed the other drill sergeants the book.

A female drill sergeant came into my face and space. "What are you smiling for, Specialist? You smile when we tell you to smile. We need to wipe that smile off your face. Get down
And PUSH!"

I stopped smiling. I learned what "getting smoked" was that day. Each branch of the military calls it something different. The Marines call it "getting bent." I was getting smoked.

The drill sergeants took turns standing over me and making me do push-ups until I was in complete and total muscle failure. Then they barked, "Flutter kicks," and I flipped over onto my back, put my hands under the backs of my legs, and lifted my legs vertically, eight to ten inches in the air, one at a time until muscle failure was again achieved. Then it was, "Push-ups!" and back to the other side on my toes doing more push-ups. Back and forth, back and forth, it seemed like hours had passed until I could NOT do ONE more. Not one. My arms, my legs, and my abs all felt like Jell-O. With sweat dripping down my face and my breath pumping, I was told to stand.

Drill Sergeant Gills came back to me. "Are you going to smile at me again?" he growled, his mirrored sunglasses STILL on.

"No, Drill Sergeant," I panted.

52

"Good." Raising his voice, he called out to the entire platoon, "We just found our new platoon guide."

I had no idea what that was. I later found out that whenever the drill sergeants weren't around, I was in charge of the forty-one other women and myself. And when the drill sergeants were there and wanted something done, they came to me first. I had to get it done. After safety, implementation was everything.

I had some leadership experience in college, chartering, starting, and leading an academic honor society, being involved in student government, and playing a year of college volleyball. But that was nothing like this. In college, everyone who "played" in those organizations wanted to be there. They were happy.

Here in basic training, many of the female trainees really didn't want to be there. They were being pushed to the depths of their physical capabilities on a constant basis. And then there was the equipment, supplies, and the facility to clean, and fire watch.

Fire watch happened every night; we had to stay awake in two-hour shifts and make sure the building did not catch on fire. If it did, the person on watch had to evacuate our unit. That made no sense to me as we had smoke alarms and a sprinkler system in the barracks. But it was part of the job. I had to assign all those duties and ensure that all tasks were implemented to the standard the drill sergeant desired.

No matter what I did, though, it wasn't good enough. And when it wasn't good enough, I got smoked. Sometimes the whole platoon was smoked *with* me, but many times, it was just me, pushing the ground while everyone else watched. When I made a

mistake, like scheduling two trainees to do the same thing at the same time, I was smoked in front of everyone. When one of the trainees made a mistake, as the leader, I was smoked for "allowing" that mistake to happen. Even when I thought everything was going OKAY, a reason was found for physical punishment. I was the platoon guide for seven out of the eight weeks. Twice, I had reprieves.

The first time, two of my trainees were really giving me a hard time. I'd direct them to do something, and they'd either ignore me or flat-out be defiant to me. Nothing I did worked, and it was affecting the morale and discipline of the rest of the platoon. It was one of the rare times that I went to the drill sergeant's office.

Both Drill Sergeant Gills and Barnes were in the office, polishing their boots. I quickly explained the situation, adding in all the other measures I had already taken. Drill Sergeant Gills didn't have his sunglasses or hat on that day, and his blue eyes crinkled at the corners as he cocked his head and studied me. He looked over at Drill Sergeant Barnes, a big, tall, broad, and imposing man of few words. They nodded to each other without saying a word, and Drill Sergeant Gills said, "Platoon Guide, we'll address this tomorrow. Dismissed."

The next day our platoon was in field operations. We marched to a forested area on the base. Wearing full gear, we were trained how to walk quietly, learning hand signals for scouting silently through the trees and the rudimentary skills of soldiering in the woods.

Drill Sergeant Gills called out the two trainees and had them stand in the position of attention. In front of the platoon, he

barked at them, "Your platoon guide tells me that you don't want to listen to what she has to say, and you are not pulling your weight."

Mentally, I cringed. *Oh, what retribution would I receive now? How would this affect the morale of the rest?*

"What the platoon guide says goes. She is my voice. When I'm not there, she is me. And when I am there, she is still *me*." Mirrored sunglasses back on, he got nose to nose with each trainee, still yelling. "Do you understand?"

"Yes, Drill Sergeant!" they shouted back in unison.

"You are both promoted to platoon guide for the day, so you can see what Specialist Mac goes through. Do you understand?"

"YES, Drill Sergeant," they shouted back.

The drill sergeant proceeded to give them task after task, and when the other trainees did not respond to them, the drill sergeant continuously smoked them: push-ups, flutter kicks, and low crawling on their bellies through the dirt.

At the final formation at the end of the day, both those trainees stood red-faced and sweaty from exertion. They were asked in front of the platoon, "Will you be giving Specialist Mac a hard time when we bring her back as platoon guide?"

"NO, Drill Sergeant," was the emphatic and immediate reply.

Drill Sergeant Gills turned back to the platoon. "Would anyone else like to be platoon guide?" Silence. "Specialist Mac?"

"Moving, Drill Sergeant!" I responded, to let him know I was stepping out of formation to report.

"You're back to platoon guide." To the platoon, he said, "I don't want to hear of any issues with this again. Understand?"

"YES, Drill Sergeant," was the collective reply.

The second time I was relieved from platoon guide duty was toward the end of the course, during bayonet and pugil stick training. We had dull rubber knives attached to the end of our M16 rifles and carried them over, under, and through an obstacle course. The course was in rough terrain, with many tree roots in the grass. About half way through the course, the toe of my combat boot lodged underneath a root. To keep from falling on the weapon I carried in front of my chest, I broke my fall to the side and twisted my left ankle. The boots provided some support, and I stood carefully before discovering I could still put a light amount of weight on my foot. I swallowed the pain and continued on.

Nearing the end of the course, I could see the drill sergeants at the end with their timers. "Finish strong!" they shouted. I picked up my speed at the end and felt another soldier push me from behind. Off-balance, I tripped. Protecting my bad left ankle, I twisted my right one and sprawled in the dirt.

I lay there for a second, assessing my pain level, both of my ankles throbbing. Could I get up? A female drill sergeant from one of the other platoons walked over to me. "Do you need a medic?"

"No, Drill Sergeant!"

"Then get up. This isn't break time." The other platoons' drill sergeants hadn't liked me since my orders for WOCS had come through and, with them, my orders for promotion. I was being promoted to a pay grade of E-5, rank of sergeant, the day of basic training graduation. Most of the drill sergeants had been in for years and were E-6s or E-7s. They were not happy for me, and I felt as if I had a target on my back.

I limped over to my platoon. The day wasn't done. We still had pugil stick training. Part of the hand-to-hand combat training we received was with a stick with a large cylinder pad at each end called a pugil stick. As we made our way over to that training area, we were told to pick our opponent. All I heard was "Mac" and "Mac" from every side around me.

As the leader, I was resented, and many of the trainees downright hated me. But they did respect me, especially since the low crawling incident with the replacement platoon guides. And sure enough, I was picked first. I could barely put weight on my ankles, but I fought through that pain to defend myself and win the fight. After all the "smokings," I was lean and strong. I took some hits but stayed on my feet.

In order to give everyone a chance to train, we could only be chosen once until the last person. The last trainee could choose anyone from the platoon and, no surprise, she picked me. I stood up, put the protective helmet back on, and the fight began. The first lunge she made hit me in the knee, and I buckled. My ankle wrenched again. It had already swollen so badly I could feel my bootlaces cutting into my skin.

I had to dig deep. I took a deep breath, sucked in the pain, and defended the blows. Then I went on the offense. It was a hard fought battle. I collapsed upon winning that last point.

I couldn't march back, and once my boot was taken off, the left ankle was swollen so badly it would not go back on. Since one of my duties was leading the platoon movements while marching and chanting some badly called cadences (the rhythmic songs repeated while running), I was relieved of platoon guide duties for the seventh of the eight weeks of training.

I implemented. Even when it hurt, even when it was difficult, I implemented.

The choices you create in the actions you take make you.

The way you react in situations that are put upon you, situations that are out of your control, defines you. The only person who could make me get back up with two sprained ankles was me.

These are the kinds of circumstances that push you and build you. Don't shy away from the opportunity to test your limits. In order to do that, you have to do something! Be deliberate about taking action and implementing.

Your potential results? You'll learn something about yourself. Even if you fail, you've learned what not to do.

At the end of basic training, the drill sergeants called me into their office. The sunglasses and hats off, they offered me a rare

smile. Their perspective? This had been their first all-female platoon. Drill Sergeant Gills admitted that, in the beginning, they were terrified of us and how this experience could have turned out for them.

They wore mirrored sunglasses to keep us from seeing the laughter in their eyes as they did the things that HAD to be done. The whole purpose of basic training was to instill discipline, the automatic response to follow orders. But for me, they knew where I was going. WOCS was one of the hardest schools, especially for a female, so it wasn't that they didn't like me or were picking on me. They smoked me every day to prepare me, physically and mentally, for that next phase of training.

In fact, Drill Sergeant Gills stood up and shook my hand. "This was the best cycle we've had, male or female. All equipment accounted for and cleaned. All duties covered. Our platoon won the Platoon of the Cycle Award, and I received Drill Sergeant of the Cycle because you made me look good. You led yourself and the platoon. Good job."

59

The P.I.L.O.T. Method

CHAPTER 6

OVERWHELM!

Drill Sergeant Gills was right. Warrant Officer Candidate School (WOCS) at Fort Rucker, Alabama, was the hardest school.

Our day started at 4:50 a.m. The only two females who had made it past "start day," Sheri and I would have to get up first and use the community bathroom. We would wear our physical fitness clothes to sleep in and would race through our morning routine in under a minute. We had to race! There were thirty men that needed to use those facilities too. And YES, the men and women shared the bathroom facilities. It was the only facility there was. And if you're thinking, *Ew*! it was probably the cleanest bathroom in Alabama. There were thirty-nine of us, all cleaning that bathroom as well as every other common area on the floor our class was responsible for.

The six weeks of grueling physical and mental training began with start day, where we were awakened in the middle of the night by alarms and foghorns. To keep things interesting, start day was a different day for each class. It might not actually be the first day. After being woken abruptly, it was outside to the training grounds for a full course of physical punishment: jumping jacks, push-ups,

flutter kicks, and rifle drills with fast sprint runs in between. Fall out (trail behind) in a run? You're set back or, worse, out of the program. There was only one standard: the warrant officer standard. On start day, our class lost five females, dropping from seven to two, due to their inability to physically keep up.

Training Command (TRADOC) regulations mandate that the course be stressful, but the stress is a tool. It is a technique to not only test the candidates but to let them know what they are made of and how far they can push themselves.

Every two weeks, the class had to change floors. Everything was cleaned, set up for inspection, packed into a duffel, and then, in a "high-intensity" move, taken outside and moved back up to a different floor. The entire time the TAC officers (Training, Advising, and Counseling), in their black shirts and black hats, stood behind us, pushing and screaming.

The TAC officers wanted us overtaxed, overtired, and overstimulated. They wanted to see what we were made of in training. This was the time to eliminate those who did not have the right stuff for handling a multimillion-dollar helicopter with lives on the line.

We lost candidates for having too many "pink slips," the derogatory form we carried in our pockets. A pink slip meant we had to spend a precious hour after the evening meal doing "time." Time equaled an hour of marching time, drill time, carrying a rubber dummy rifle through the quad area. The rest of us would use that time for hygiene (yes, even that time was limited) and organizing our rooms: rolling our socks, spit polishing our boots to the expected mirror finish, and even taking nail polish remover and

removing every lot number stamped onto the bottom of every deodorant or shampoo bottle. Everything was positioned to within a fraction of an inch. It was attention to detail, and the work was never finished. There was always something more to do, and if you were caught polishing your personal area of inspection during study time, your life became miserable very quickly.

A pink slip could be filled out for any misstep. In six weeks, I had one pink slip. I had neglected to come to the position of attention when I called "Attention" to the floor as a TAC officer stepped into that space. I quickly corrected, but he got in my face and demanded my pink slip.

I did my time.

The superiors wanted to see how we would perform under pressure. Would we crack? Some did. Would we succumb to the overwhelm and never accomplish anything of value by doing most tasks at a lower-quality level? Some did. Or would we properly prioritize and complete the appropriate tasks in the allotted time? Most did. And because we were a class, we helped those struggling the best we could. We polished their boots next to our own. We cleaned others' living spaces. We checked drawers that had to be organized just so. We helped with everything but studying and physical fitness.

From this training, I learned how to survive and thrive with overwhelm. You see, if you focus on all the things you have to do, it is mentally overwhelming. Your brain fries from processing all those uncompleted tasks. We learned to be completely present to the moment, to what we were doing, to complete it and then ask ourselves, "What's next?"

63

Contrary to popular belief, you can only do one task at a time, at least at a high level of performance.

Your brain can only focus 100 percent on one thing at a time, and when we divide our focus, we don't do anything well. Ask yourself, "What's urgent and important for me to accomplish NEXT?" There are urgent things, and there are always important things. But doing what is urgent and important first should keep you out of trouble. This becomes really important as you lead yourself through greater levels of responsibility.

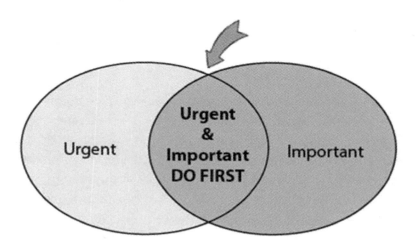

It is way too EASY to just be busy. Ask anyone, and they will tell you they are busy. But are they effective? Are they productive? Are they accomplishing tasks?

I believe in being a life-long learner. But there are professional students (those in school or out of school) who take courses, classes, and seminars but never put what they learn into practice.

They are in analysis paralysis, having to study more, waiting for that perfect knowledge or point to occur to drive them into action.

Don't let this be YOU. When you learn something that aligns with your goals, take action on it. There is never a more perfect time than right now. Turn off the TV, the music, and the phone (gasp), and focus 100 percent on something that is urgent and important. It's probably something that you've put off and haven't done yet. What are you waiting for? Get it done NOW!

And when it's done, go to **pilotmethod.com** and comment on the "Get It Done!" blog post linked from the home page. I want to know what you have accomplished. I'll celebrate with you!

The P.I.L.O.T. Method

CHAPTER 7

PRACTICE MAKES PERMANENT

I graduated WOCS and moved straight into flight school, called Initial Entry Rotary Wing (IERW) training. Aeromedical classes, aerodynamics classes, and training on the systems of a UH-1H Huey helicopter were first. Then we were in a cockpit mockup trainer learning how to start up and shut down the Huey. It was exciting to finally be in the training, but it was also daunting. You see, I wasn't a mechanic-chick!

Because we had to learn the systems quickly, there wasn't time for a lot of questions. I was expected to catch up on my own time. After classes all day, I went to study group and then studied for hours after that, memorizing every component—where it was, what it did, what happened if it failed—and the corresponding emergency procedure.

Occasionally I had to call my dad. "What does a hydraulic pump do?" I'd ask. Or, "What does a step down transformer do?" As the only female in the class, it was a constant struggle and frustration for me to keep up.

67

Then it was time to go out to the flight line at Lowe Army Airfield, Fort Rucker. We were all so excited to finally get to fly! When I walked into the room, I found out I was paired up with Ryan for my "stick buddy." Student pilots were never alone with an instructor. One student pilot would fly, while the other student pilot would observe from the back seat, serving the duties of a crew chief and ensuring the aircraft was cleared to turn. I walked over to the instructor's table to meet a DAC (Department of Army Civilian) named

Buck. As I stood in front of this older, leather-skinned man, he looked up at me, rolled his eyes, and sarcastically said, "Oh great."

I knew I was in trouble. It quickly became clear to me that he didn't agree with women flying helicopters, but legally he couldn't fail me because of that. He could sure scream at me while I flew, though, and try to make me fail. And that's what happened. I was trying to learn to fly a UH-1H Huey while this guy made every minute in the cockpit a living hell.

Of everything that I struggled with, the physicality of flying was the hardest. Flying a helicopter was not like flying a plane and not even close to driving a car or anything else I had ever experienced.

Each foot operates independently on the pedals. Your right hand is on the cyclic, and not only are you controlling the pitch of the rotor blades and the movement of the helicopter with your cyclic, you're also controlling the microphone with a finger trigger and keeping your left hand on the collective for power. You're on the radio; you're talking on a lip microphone with ground or air

traffic control; you're keeping a constant scan of the instruments and the terrain obstacles outside the multiple windows.

It's multitasking on anabolic steroids.

The first thing you learn while training in the actual helicopter is to hover. Hovering is the hardest part of piloting a helicopter. You're fighting winds while the rotor blades are creating their own wind to give you lift, and it can be a bumpy, unstable ride. It requires a gentle touch to hover, and it needs soft and slow movements. Do you know how hard it is to fly soft and slow when someone is screaming in your helmet headset? "You're not good enough! What makes you think you can do this? A monkey can fly this, and you can't!"

I couldn't relax enough to hover. As soon as my hands touched the aircraft's controls, Buck's berating began. And my doubts would creep in. *What was I thinking*? No matter how much I prepared and committed to not let it get to me, I'd clench my hand. I'd tense up, and the helicopter would start swinging, a little to the right, overcorrecting to the left, overcorrecting back to the right—until the body of the helicopter swung under the rotor blades like the pendulum of a clock. That was bad! And Buck would snatch the controls from me, screaming, "I have the controls" and berating me again. It felt like an endless cycle.

Ryan, my stick buddy, totally got it. We hovered and did fun maneuvers with him, while I was stuck in the back seat watching. Ryan knew Buck had singled me out for intimidation, and Ryan would pat me on the shoulder and say, "You're going to get it," while I fought back tears.

69

That was bad, but it was the absolute worst being the only female in my class, coming closer to the end of that phase of training, and still not able to hover. I was last. LAST! I'd always come in first or maybe second in everything I'd tried. And I was close to failing at this. But I refused to quit. I would not quit.

I kept showing up. I had no idea how I was going to pass, but I knew I was still where I was supposed to be. I believed I was going to make it through even though I didn't know how.

Then, on a Monday morning close to the end of the training cycle, I walked in to the briefing room, and at Buck's table was a younger, active duty Army substitute instructor. My spirits lifted. I had hope! There was a chance. This could be the HOW I was hoping for. I walked up to the table, and he was flipping through the pages of my grade sheets. They were not pretty. I wasn't making a great first impression.

He looked up at me. I smiled and said, "How're ya doing?"

"What's the deal?" He pointed down at the flight records.

I burst into tears. "I'm trying really hard. Then Buck yells at me and calls me stupid and says that a monkey can fly better than me!" The words came faster and faster, and hot tears slid down my cheeks. (Did I mention crying in uniform is REALLY BAD?)

The substitute cut me off. "Please stop!"

I sucked it up and dried my face with the back of my hands.

"Do you want this?" he asked.

Did I want this? The smart aleck in me wanted to say, "Duh! Why would I have put up with weeks and weeks of this verbal abuse if I didn't want this?" But all I said was, "Oh, yes."

"Let's do it!" Ryan and I followed him out to the helicopter. He was patient and showed me how to hold my right elbow braced against my body so my hand could be smoother and more stable on the controls. One simple tip, and I was up in the air at last! I could do it!

This warrant officer substitute taught me more in that week than the other instructor had taught me during the rest of the class.

Final exam week arrived. I was able to pass—*in last place*.

That taught me an important lesson. Practice doesn't make perfect. That is a myth. Ask any athlete. If you practice something incorrectly, it's not perfect.

Practice makes permanent!

How you practice is how you'll perform. The large majority of my practice time was with Buck, doing the maneuvers incorrectly because he didn't have the patience or the willingness to teach me. I'd picked up all these bad habits from doing the essential skills incorrectly for so long that practice had made it permanent. I had to learn something different to practice, break my habits, and start relearning correctly. That is a lot harder than learning it correctly from the beginning.

How you practice is how you show up. If you're an actor or actress, you read your lines as if you're in front of an audience every time. If you're going into a job interview, you practice answering the questions as if you're looking that interviewer in the eye. You give what you do your all because that is how you're showing up for whatever your next challenge is.

There is no do-over in your life!

CHAPTER 8

READY, FIRE, ADJUST YOUR AIM

Author's Note: To help emphasize some of the PILOT Method truths, I've interviewed other pilots, helicopter and fixed-wing, to share their stories of leading themselves in life and flight.

It was early 1971 in Vietnam, and Army Warrant Officer Doug Petersen was assigned to the 45th Medical Company "Dustoff." Doug was "first up" one day, meaning his crew and aircraft would receive the first call for a medical extraction. The radio call came for an urgent pickup about thirty miles to the east. It would be a hoist mission because of the terrain. (A hoist mission involves hovering over the jungle and lowering a cable down with a jungle penetrator extraction board and harness.) Doug and his copilot ran out to the UH1-D in the first-up pad on the heliport. The crew chief and medic were in a full run too. All had strapped on the thick armor plates to hopefully protect them from bullets. In a matter of four minutes from the sound of the alarm, they were hovering for takeoff.

Doug's crew called the various firebases to make sure there wasn't any artillery firing along the intended route. It was clear. A few kilometers away, they established contact via radio with the

unit on the ground. The crew asked the ground unit about enemy contact and the direction of the last engagement. The ground unit relayed the information and their position.

"Prepare to pop smoke."

Flying at a safe altitude, Doug assessed the terrain and probable approach path. "Pop smoke. We'll identify the color." Doug saw purple smoke filtering from the jungle canopy.

"Goofy grape."

Clicking the radio frequency, Doug replied, "Roger."

Doug conducted one final crew briefing upon approach for the pickup of the injured soldier. Descending below the safe small-arms fire altitude, the Huey hovered over the treetops and was guided to the vicinity of the purple smoke. Suspended over the trees and in constant radio contact with the unit on the ground, Doug knew they were close.

The crew chief and medic leaned over the sides of the aircraft, looking for the ground unit. The hoist was ready to lower the jungle penetrator to pick up the injured. Focused on the directions from the radio operator NS maneuvering the Huey just over the trees, all eyes searched the ground below. Suddenly, the crack of an AK-47 became the loudest sound.

Over the intercom, the crew chief shouted, "We're taking fire!" "Enemy at 5:00. We flew right over the top of them!" the copilot shouted.

The Huey started taking hits, the emergency panel lights lit up, and the master caution alarm whined. The aircraft was losing oil pressure; an oil line was hit. Doug was certain fuel, and possibly hydraulic fluid as well, was leaking.

The aircraft was still at tree top and needed a place to land before the engine quit. There was no choice. Doug quickly banked left, pulled power, and dropped the nose to gain some airspeed. It was imperative to get out of there quickly.

The customary distress call was made. "Mayday. Mayday! Dustoff 34 is going down!" Doug gave the location. A couple thousand meters away was a clearing, and Doug headed toward it, expecting the engine to quit at any moment.

Doug wasn't really worried about anything other than getting away from the enemy fire and getting his crew on the ground. Fortunately, there was some air cover with a couple of Cobra helicopter gunships flying around overhead. This provided some comfort. Within twenty minutes or so, infantry APC (armored personnel carriers) came from the west and set up a perimeter around the damaged helicopter.

Doug and the crew walked around the aircraft to survey the damage. Fuel and oil were leaking out from several places.

Looking around some more, they noticed that the glass of a gauge in the instrument panel was shattered. Upon closer inspection, they realized one of the rounds the aircraft took came through from the back of the instrument and, based on the trajectory, stopped just short of hitting the copilot.

The crew took all the sensitive equipment out and waited to be picked up. They then climbed aboard the helicopter that had been sent to get them and returned to their home base. Once there, Doug got another aircraft and headed back to complete the mission. After all, there was an injured soldier still waiting to be picked up.

As the crew flew back out, a Chinook came from the opposite direction, with the damage swaying below as a sling load. They picked up the wounded soldier, transported him back, and completed the mission—for that day.

As a pilot, we're prepared for the circumstances and challenges that may arise, but more than that, we are prepared to adjust. We plan and think through every possibility and then move forward with action toward completing our mission.

People want everything to be perfect, but it doesn't happen.

I've known people who say things like:

"When I make this amount of money, I'll be happy."
"When I have this promotion, I'll feel fulfilled."
"When I lose this ten pounds, I'll become content."

You can't start from any other place than where you are right now. The perfect place to start is where you are.

I don't know who said this, but it is so true:

> **"You don't have to be great to start,
> but you have to start to be great."**

76

Doug didn't scrutinize every action, sit back, and wait to start. There was a mission to be done. When medevac is called, it means there is an injured soldier (or soldiers) on the ground. To not show up is to let them down; to not be there for an extraction means someone could die.

Here is where so many of us get stuck. It's in the AIMING of your life. We get stuck in the analysis paralysis! We research, research, compile information, research some more, stall, and delay because the plan is not perfect enough. Have we covered all the details, every possible contingency? Wait! Let's look at the research again.

Sound familiar?

Using research as an excuse to delay and not make a decision does NOT get the mission accomplished. And your LIFE is your Mission.

Consider Doug's mission. He knew the general area where the injured were waiting. They had a procedure called "popping a smoke grenade" to signal their position. They did everything feasible to prevent coming into contact with enemy fire, yet they still did.

Instead of over-controlling, overanalyzing, and micro managing the situation, they "fired," taking action, flying the mission, and then adjusting their aim to the unforeseen circumstances.

Doesn't this happen in life? We are living our life in what we think is our plan when—BAM!—something happens that forces us to adjust.

The timeline adjusts.
The plan shifts.
And sometimes, the whole DREAM changes.

It's okay when this happens. It's normal to have these detours.

I've had a few major detours myself, like...being in the middle of a divorce during flight school.

I was in the instrument phase of flight training. We were doing simulator work, in a small, dark box with very few visual cues, on hydraulics to simulate movements. There is a small lag between the controls to the movements. Vertigo is common; in fact, one of the skills we learn is to trust our instruments even when in vertigo, so we can recover.

Every morning in that simulator, I got nauseated to the point of having to stop and be sick. After four days in a row, the instructor sent me to the doctor. Pilots do not like to go to the doctor because usually that means we won't get to fly. When the doctor found nothing wrong on the physical exam, I was sent out for blood tests and lab work. Unexpectedly, I was pregnant—and not just a little pregnant but almost four months along!

I was the only female in my class, in the middle of a divorce, and pregnant. Do you think this was an adjustment in my timeline? A shift in my plan? A change in priorities? I was placed in medical

hold and had to watch everyone I had gone through WOCS with pass me by. I had to adjust my timeline.

I also had to adjust physically, as toward the end of my pregnancy I was put on complete bed rest. In nearly three months, I gained close to fifty pounds. It was a huge change from the lean and buff candidate I had been.

Success isn't "Ready, Aim, Fire" toward your target.

It is:

Ready (Get prepared),
Fire (Take action),
Adjust Your Aim (Make necessary adjustments to complete your mission).

The P.I.L.O.T. Method

CHAPTER 9

EVEN WHEN YOU DON'T WANT TO

"They want a plane to divert into Rota," the navigator yelled as the last engine rumbled to life.

"WHAT?" Major Kimberly Olson, a command pilot in the United
States Air Force, barked over the intercom, causing the crew to flinch.

She drew a deep breath. "And?" There was always an "and" when being diverted.

"The plane is to wait for two F-16s to get fixed and drag them home across the Atlantic." The navigator's voice was hoarse and tight.

Silence filled the cockpit as they chewed on this news. Major Olson watched her young crew members physically sink into themselves. They were all tired, anxious to get home, and worn out from sleeping in desert tents for the last 127 nights.

But this was their job; they were tanker drivers.

Official military description: fly the modified Boeing 707 airplane designed to perform inflight refueling.
Pilot description: pass gas at 25,000 feet.

The tanker's motto is: "Can't kick ass without tanker gas." This is especially true for fighter jets, which need thousands of pounds of aviation gas to fly, fight, and get home safely.

"How long?" she asked, expressing the crew members' thoughts.

"They want to know if we can wait two hours for spare parts," the navigator growled.

For a moment, she studied the somber faces of her four crew members. They had been a team for over two years, and as their aircraft commander and leader, Major Olson knew all their wives, kids, dogs, and even some of their parents. They had traversed over land and sea, bounced around thunderstorms, and staggered out of bars together. They had logged hundreds of hours planning, flying, and debriefing. They knew their strengths and weaknesses. A last-minute diversion that extended time away from home was definitely a weakness.

The military prides itself on planning, but when those plans meet reality, well, to use aviation lingo, things can get "Foxtrot Uniform."

"Say no," someone whispered on the intercom. More silence.

"Tell them yes," she surrendered slowly.

"Shit," came another voice. Major Olson gritted her teeth and swallowed a response.

"Engine shutdown checklist." She turned to the copilot. He was lost in thought, probably imagining holding his newborn son, now asleep some eleven time zones away.

"Engine shutdown checklist, Copilot. Now!" Major Olson repeated sharply.

He jumped, nodded, and began the drill.

Cutting the engines, the crew began the tasks of re-filing their flight plan from Saudi Arabia to Spain and readying the cargo bay for the spare part. After waiting an hour in the desert heat, a truck pulled up and handed the crew chief a carton that was no bigger than a shoebox.

"We delayed for that?" her copilot asked no one in particular.

The usual banter during takeoff and climb-out to their cruising altitude was gone, and she knew the complaining would start soon. "Pilots aren't happy unless they are whining" is the common joke in flight rooms, but Kimberly also knew her crew was not happy with her or the mission.

As they leveled off, the copilot turned to Major Olson and said, "I sure miss my son."

"I know you do. We'll get home soon," Major Olson answered, half believing it herself. Broken fighter jets, especially F-16s, had a way of staying broken, and once their tanker was partnered with a

two-ship of fighters, it was stuck with them until they coasted into U.S. air space. Tankers were their lifeline home. This was the reason tanker crews rarely bought beer at the base bar. It was also the reason they could spend another week away from their families.

Being the aircraft commander was easy. There were checklists outlining who performed what task in the cockpit. There were clear military chains of command. There were regulations governing flying operations, and when they were not on real-world missions, they were training. Theirs was a well-disciplined and talented flight crew.

Major Olson had the aircraft commander part down, but it was the leadership piece that gave her the most challenge. She felt challenged all right, for at this juncture, she wanted to pop her copilot for his solemn mood. She wanted to tell her navigator to shut up about how screwed they were and how they would never get home.

Teaching moments and true leadership really do present themselves at interesting times, even at 25,000 feet.

"Pilot's checking off, Co (short for copilot, pronounced Coe). You got the aircraft."

"Roger," he acknowledged, still sulking.

Major Olson walked past the small box to the back of the cargo compartment to stretch her legs as well as her mind. A part of her wanted to kick the box that represented the delay in returning to their families. But she had a choice: join them or lead

them. And leading can be lonely; it sets you apart and distances you from those you care about.

Kimberly pulled out the picture of her twelve-month-old, kissed it, and whispered, "See you soon, son."

Being a mother, aircraft commander, and leader was indeed an interesting mix. Sometimes she intertwined the mothering and leadership skills together.

Climbing back into the seat, she slapped the copilot playfully on the shoulder. "Spain! Have any of you been to Spain?"

Silence.

"I thought as much. Nav, get on that computer of yours and tell us what waits for this crew in Spain." Major Olson used a voice she usually reserved for her son.

For the next four hours, they learned about their new destination and adventures. By the time Major Olson and her crew rolled to a stop at the Spanish airfield, heads were higher, laughter echoed in the cockpit, and a cool evening breeze greeted them as the hatch slowly opened.

Climbing out of the cockpit seat, she came face to face with the fighter maintenance OIC (officer in charge). Pumping her hand, he rambled, "Captain, they are so glad to see you. You're our ride home. They are so ready to be out of here."

"Is the bird fixed?" she asked, surprised.

"Tomorrow morning, I promise," he replied, kissing the spare part carton the crew chief handed him. Kimberly rolled her eyes. Her crew watched and waited.

"Look, LT, my crew is tired, they're hungry, and they need a shower. Can you make that happen?" she said as she winked at her crew.

"Oh, hell yeah!" the OIC's Texas twang rang. "Sarge, get these good people to billeting and have the mess hall ready the meal...in an hour?"

Major Olson nodded, chuckling at his enthusiasm. "Come on, men. Spain awaits." She jumped down to the ramp.

But Spain would have to wait even longer. True to the OIC's word, the fighters were fixed by morning. The maintenance team had worked all night. Within twelve hours of their arrival, they were airborne again, en route to home.

What Major Olson and her crew would learn on the flight back home was that fifteen military troops had been relying on them to bring that spare part and get them home safely. And connected to those fifteen were another twenty-five wives and children anxiously awaiting their return. Nearly forty-five people were relying on that small carton.

As some of the troops rotated through the cockpit to enjoy the view and thank them for the lift home, Major Olson's crew seemed to mature.

"Howdy, ma'am," boomed the Texas maintenance OIC as he entered the cockpit, tipping an imaginary cowboy hat. His knuckles were bloodied and scarred, and the entire crew noticed.

She raised an eyebrow. "What does the other guy look like?" she teased.

He shrugged and joked about fighter jets biting your hand when you work on their engines.

"That must smart," she said.

He furrowed his brow and leaned forward. "Not as much as letting down my team." His voice was serious.

Major Olson watched her copilot blink twice. He then reached across the cockpit to place his hand gently over the OIC's scars. "Tex, it was our honor to serve you."

Tex blushed and drawled a long, "Shucks."

Major Olson suppressed a huge grin and sighed proudly.

There are always going to be things you don't want to do.

Kimberly's crew didn't want to extend their time; they wanted to go home to see their families. As the commander, and as a mother wanting to be home with her son, Kimberly herself struggled, thoughtfully choosing the right action even when it was difficult.

Not everything in life is fun by any means. I don't know anyone who looks forward to paying bills and doing housework,

and some people don't even like going to work. Yet, it is all part of life. How you handle the things you don't like to do is a great reflection on your work ethic. Do complaints come out of your mouth whenever you are faced with doing something you don't necessarily enjoy, or do you just forge ahead and get it done with the same tenacity as you would something you do enjoy?

When I was in high school, I played basketball, and despite being vertically challenged, I was on varsity for three years. (It was a small school.) In my senior year, we had a junior, Roseanne, who was an All-State player. One day, Roseanne looked at me and said, "Do you ever stop complaining?"

I was stunned. I didn't even HEAR myself complaining! Was I complaining? It was a complete shift of awareness. I started to hear the things I was saying, and sure enough, I didn't like what I heard. It was negative, and it was not attractive. I forced myself to change. Every time a thought popped into my head that was critical, complaining, or whiny, I shut it down. I visually pressed the delete button in my head. It did NOT serve me. It did not have to be ME. I could be positive. It took willpower and perspective on life to change my attitude. It wasn't easy.

In order to succeed at anything, we have to do even the hard things that we don't want to do. Sometimes the hardest tasks are the most important ones. They generally appear harder than they are because we allow ourselves to feel overwhelmed by them, which leads to procrastination.

The hard part is when we're unmotivated, uninspired, and distracted. That is when we need to kick ourselves in the rear and say, "Suck it up, Buttercup" and get it done. It is the mark of a true

champion to complete those less favorable tasks with a smile on your face.

Eat That Frog by Brian Tracy is one of my favorite books. (It's short!) In it, Brian explains why you should take the most difficult, most dreaded, and most cumbersome task and do it first. He uses the analogy: If the task is to eat a frog, do it first. Get it over with, and then everything else gets easier after that. That's a lesson I put into practice now on a daily basis, especially when that "frog" falls into my "important and urgent" category.

Remember, the longer you procrastinate, the more stress it will bring on, especially when the tasks are attached to a deadline. Not only will it bring on more stress, but it can also result in less-than-quality work. It can erode your self-confidence by undermining your belief in yourself and your ability to accomplish things. It is worth the effort to actively improve upon preventing procrastinating habits.

Remember, the things we resist doing the most are more than likely the things we should be doing first and that generally yield the greatest reward.

Stop being your own worst enemy!

Get it done!

The P.I.L.O.T. Method

LEADERSHIP

CHAPTER 10

CAN LEADERSHIP · COMMUNICATE

Author's Note: All aviators know to Aviate, Navigate, and Communicate. They are the three things a pilot must ALWAYS do while flying. In the Leadership section, these are three foundational Pillars of Leadership. They work together to enable you to lead yourself (and others). Take one away, and the other two suffer. You CAN Lead yourself. Then you'll FLY: First Lead Yourself!

There is no such thing as a quiet pilot. There is a nonstop patter with an aircrew. While planning any flight or mission, there is communication:

The scheduler notifies the pilot.
Operations communicates the mission profile.
A flight plan is filed.
A weather report is received.
A risk assessment matrix is completed.
The safety check is completed.
The aircraft is preflighted.
The mission is briefed.
The crew is briefed.
The passengers are briefed.

Of course, some of these tasks may be split between pilots, and on the commercial side, many of these tasks are completed by a team to support the airline's ultimate goal: to get the passengers transported safely. But no matter what tasks are delegated or conducted by support staff, the ultimate responsibility falls on the pilot in command, the officer in charge, the captain. The lead pilot may decide to have more fuel added or to recheck a component after maintenance, all while maintaining communication on how that will affect the mission's time on target.

In a cockpit, it can get even noisier. In the Black Hawk, it was a steady stream in the run-up sequence. As an example, during starting engines (from the Operator's Manual TM-1-1520-237-10 Change 10):

One pilot would read through the checklist, while the other pilot performed the task. "Engine fuel system selectors as required, XFD, for first start of the day," would be called out.

The other pilot would check that lever to make sure it was in the correct position. "Check," was called out to verify.

"Engine ignition switch ON."
"Check," was the reply as it was moved and verified.
"Gust lock caution light OFF."
"Check."
"Fire guard posted."
"Check," was called out after making a visual confirmation.
"Rotor blades clear."
"Check."
And so on.

Ready for takeoff? In addition to internal communication among the pilots, crew, and passengers, add in the radio calls to ground control, the tower, and the air traffic control center. Communication is key.

Since there is no autopilot in the Black Hawk, a positive three-way transfer of the controls is required.

"You have the controls?"

"I have the controls." The other pilot confirmed that he or she physically had his or her hands on the controls.

"You have the controls" was the reply to relinquish the controls.

Someone has to be on the controls. There is no autopilot in the Black Hawk, and there is no autopilot in your life.

It's WHAT you say in your life, your job, and your business; it's what you say to your family, your friends, your coworkers, and your boss. It all has an impact.

In order to communicate well with others and effectively have your voice heard, you need to develop those skills. The way in which you communicate is often used by others to determine how valid your point is and if you present yourself in a professional manner.

If you believe that your verbal communication skills could use some improvement, here are some tips:

> • **Thought**. Before you ever open your mouth to speak, it is highly recommended that you think first. Rather than speaking the first thought that pops into your mind, you should take a moment to carefully consider what you intend to say. This will help prevent anything you say from reflecting poorly on you and your message.

> • **Clarity**. Many individuals are unwilling to continue listening to someone if they have to work to figure out what that person is trying to say. This is why the clearer you are when you speak and express your ideas, the more open individuals will be to hearing everything that you have to say. It's how you say it.

> • **Confidence**. The more certain you are about the message you are sharing, the more receptive people will be to what

you are saying. When you speak with confidence, remember to carefully choose your words, pay attention to the tone of your voice, maintain eye contact with your audience, and take note of your body language.

• **Friendliness**. Individuals who speak with a friendly tone and smile throughout their conversation are often listened to more attentively than those who don't. The reason is that we tend to be drawn to individuals who are friendly because they are more enjoyable to be around, and they also tend to make us feel better about ourselves.

It's also what ISN'T being said.

A large amount of our daily communication is conducted through nonverbal behavior. In a typical day, we respond to nonverbal cues that we receive from others. These behaviors include facial expressions, gestures, postures, eye movements, and different voice tones. Many of these communications are so subtle that we are not aware they are occurring, but subconsciously we respond.

Here are some of the most common nonverbal techniques:

• **Facial Expressions**. The expressions that we create using our facial muscles account for the largest amount of nonverbal communication throughout the day. With a simple smile or frown, we can relate many of the different emotions that we are feeling at any particular moment. Since most facial expressions for emotions are similar across cultures, we are able to express our emotions and

97

recognize the same ones in others regardless of any language barrier.

• **Gestures**. This is another great example of how we communicate without using words. Using gestures such as waving, pointing, and indicating numbers can express a multitude of verbal equivalents. From waving a simple hello to someone across the room, or indicating that your child is two-years old, gestures can be used to transmit a large amount of information.

• **Posture**. Our body posture can be used to convey different defensive responses. These include the crossing of our arms and legs. This type of communication can be used to express our displeasure with someone or something or to keep people from approaching us. The military taught me to convey confidence just by standing straight with my shoulders back and chest out.

• **Eye Gaze**. Looking, staring, and blinking are nonverbal behaviors that we express through our eyes. When people experience something they like, their rate of blinking will increase. Our eye gaze can also be used to indicate emotions such as hostility, attraction, and interest.

• **Appearance**. Many do not think that the way we present ourselves is a method of communicating, but they are wrong. Our choice of clothing, colors, and hairstyles can be used to represent our particular mood and can alter the physiological reactions that others have toward us based on our appearance.

Communication requires a two-way transfer. Someone talks, and the other person has to listen. Are you an effective listener? Do you really know what effective listening entails? Research shows that only 25 percent of us listen effectively. To be an effective listener, you must not only listen with your ears, but you must use your eyes as well to pick up obvious and not so obvious body language. To be an effective listener, you must be able to absorb the information being delivered to you and show that you are interested and listening but also have the ability to give relevant feedback.

Most people believe they are effective listeners, but at the same time, most will admit they only truly listen attentively when the topic is something of interest to them. The true test of an effective listener is whether or not you listen when the subject of discussion is less important to you.

The benefits of being an effective listener can include:

- Receiving clear information from the speaker
- More trust from those you deal with
- Less conflict
- Insight on how and what motivates those you deal with
- A stronger commitment from those you deal with

When you listen to others attentively, you show them that they matter and that what they have to say is important to you. Effective listening promotes a win-win situation because you are, in a sense, teaching the skill by your behavior/actions and are more likely to get the same consideration back when you are speaking.

As pilots, our communication is proactive. To lead yourself (and others), you need to be proactive. In communication, this simply means answering questions before they're asked. By acting in a proactive manner, you are able to recognize problems before they turn into larger issues. You can also improve your relationships and handle any problems before they occur.

There are two simple keys that will help you improve your basic communication skills:

- **Attention**! Get the attention of the person or people you are planning to communicate with first. Too often, we start talking and the person or people we are speaking to are not on the same page as we are. Make sure they are connected with you through body language, verbal acknowledgment, and eye contact.

- **Speak clearly**! Did I express that clearly enough? Keep your voice and tone alive. You don't want to bore or put to sleep the person or people you are speaking with, so don't speak like you are reading a bedtime story—unless of course that is your intent. Make sure your facial expressions match the message you are trying to send. Having a "blank" face (no emotion) is boring and bound to not get you much attention. Express as much through your facial and body language as you do through your voice.

Is your communication really connecting? Is it clear? Is it concise?

Effective communication is one of my three Pillars of Leadership because you can't lead yourself (or others) without it. Communication affects everything.

Communication is an area that almost everyone has struggled with at some point in life, but with some practice and experience, you can be well-prepared.

The P.I.L.O.T. Method

CHAPTER II

CAN LEADERSHIP · AVIATE

Author's Note: If you are reading this and wondering, "How is Elizabeth going to make me aviate?" you should know that Aviate = Action. Although we covered action in depth in the section on implementation, there is a part of aviating and taking action that I saved just for this chapter. Remember that these three Pillars of Leadership work together for you to lead yourself (and others). Take one away, and the other two suffer. You CAN Lead yourself. Then you'll FLY: First Lead Yourself!

Pilots do not sit back and wait for the aircraft to do something. They aviate. They fly their aircraft. They make it happen. What does that mean to you? It means you are intentionally and fully present and fully alert to what you are doing as you do it.

Imagine you are in the front car of a big amusement park roller coaster, and you can make it do almost anything you want. There is no track. You can fly it fast, slow, high, or low and turn right or left. You control where it goes and what it does. That is the experience closest to flying a helicopter.

There is a lot of action going on with just flying. Imagine you're controlling the power to the engines with your left hand and the power to the tail rotor (in models that have one) with each foot on a pedal. Your right hand is on the cyclic, controlling the pitch of the rotor blades and your movements forward, backward, or side to side. At the same time, you're scanning your instruments and looking out the windows for obstacles. All the while, you're communicating on the internal communication system and through the radios for air traffic or the mission profile.

All of this requires a pilot to be in a heightened state of being present. I would fly a two-hour mission in cold weather, and by the end of my flight time, I would be drenched in sweat—and it wasn't from the heater!

In chapter seven, the truth of "practice makes permanent" was shared. Here, it's more about being fully present in your moment.

Buck Burney was the new Detachment (DET) commander 125th Fighter Wing Detachment 1 at Homestead Air Reserve Base, Florida. The unit's mission was to provide the Continental NORAD Region commander a rapid response to invasions of the sovereign airspace of the United States and respond with appropriate defense measures against all hostile actions directed at the people and property of the United States (per fl.ang.af.mil/units/index.asp).

Buck was in charge of the two F-15s ready to scramble on board with missiles within five minutes of any alert. It is a difficult task during normal circumstances, but this was during the 1996 shoot down of the two Brothers to the Rescue pilots by Cuba.

In February 1996, two Brothers to the Rescue pilots were shot down and killed by the Cuban Air Force. A third pilot escaped. Despite the fact that the Brothers to the Rescue planes were outside Cuban airspace, the Cuban Air Force ordered a MiG-29 and a MiG-23 to attack.

The Cuban MiGs were loaded with bombs and short-range missiles. The Brothers were flying two Cessna 337s, a civilian plane known for safety. Over transmission radio, the Cuban Air Force pilots were heard celebrating as the Cessnas were shot down very near the U.S. fishing vessel Tri-Liner as well as the cruise ship Majesty of the Seas.

"The other one is destroyed; the other one is destroyed. Homeland or death...you bastards! The other one is also down."

Buck's DET was immediately activated in light of this emergency, going from two F-15s and four missiles to fifteen F-15s and eight missiles at the highest state of alert. War was imminent.

And with Florida's close proximity to Cuba, the situation could change at any moment.

It was during this time that Jill, a maintenance chief from the base in Jacksonville, called about the launch of a new program called "Young Heroes" that would issue the "Medal of Courage" to kids who were dying or suffering from critical illnesses. Buck was requested to present the first medals and answer questions at the elementary school.

Buck refused. As a new commander, there was too much going on; the op tempo was too high.

Jill called again and implored Buck, explaining their willingness to schedule the event around his schedule. Buck wanted to say, "No." He intended to say, "No," but ended up saying, "Yes." He then put it out of his mind to focus on the situations at his detachment.

When the day came, Buck flew to Jacksonville International Airport and used a staff car to go to the elementary school in Ponte Vedra Beach for the ceremony. At the elementary school, Buck would issue the first award to Bobby, a young student with cancer. In fact, as the principal took Buck through the school, she explained that although the district policy was "no hats" for the students, because there were several students with cancer, hats and scarfs were being allowed. Buck walked through the halls, his mind still occupied with the work to be done at Homestead.

The medal was awarded, and upon completion of the ceremony, the principal asked Buck to talk to a few of the classes. After agreeing, Buck was taken into Bobby's classroom. Thinking

he'd be answering questions about flying or the Cuban Missile Crisis, he stood in the front of the room. A little girl with pigtails raised her hand and asked, "Why is Bobby a hero?"

Concerned about saying the right thing, about answering the question perfectly, Buck talked about Bobby having the courage to face his illness and to go through a difficult thing that most adults hurt through.

Looking at his watch, Buck had turned to go when he felt a small tug on the back of his flight suit. It was little Bobby, his big brown eyes peering out from under the brim of his baseball cap. "Thank you for giving me my award, Sir."

Buck's eyes welled with tears, and a lump formed in his throat. So concerned was he about his job that he forgot to be fully present for the life of this child.

It was one of those defining moments in life when Buck realized he'd shown up, but he had NOT done his best. He wasn't present to the joy of the situation. He was walking fast from one task to the next and not being present in the journey.

Have you ever done that? Have you been so busy at a task that you weren't fully aware of anything else in the process? Have you ever focused on something while driving and then realized when you got home that you had no idea how you got there?

Living life in focus means being conscious of what you are doing so you do it with complete awareness. Maintaining your focus can be one of the hardest things to do, but if you are trying to achieve a particular goal, staying focused on that goal is the only

way you will achieve it. Dividing your focus will cause you to give your particular goal only a portion of the attention it deserves. In order to achieve your goals, it is critical to your success that you stay focused.

Here are some strategies to keep you focused:

• **Define your goal**. (We'll be going through more of this in the next chapter: "Navigate." See how the Pillars of Leadership are interconnected?) Your goal should be as specific as possible and include a defined outcome and strategy that will help you execute your agenda in the best manner possible.

• **Take action toward that goal**. Only take action on one item at a time. Contrary to popular belief, multitasking is not good for you!

• **Eliminate distractions**. Turn off the phone (or put it on airplane mode for a while). Check your social media and email on your schedule, around other tasks. Turn off the sound on the notifications to prevent checking.

• **Put tasks on your calendar**. What is on your calendar receives your time.

• **Focus on what is working**. That way you won't become distracted by focusing all of your attention on what is not working.

• **Celebrate your successes**. Any milestone of achievement along the way is a reason to reward yourself.

• Surround yourself with a supportive team.

By following these suggestions, I am confident that you will be able to focus your attention where it needs to be. Maintaining focus is a learned skill, but if you utilize the strategies I have listed above, staying focused may become somewhat easier.

Aviating your life is about being present and fully focused. When you communicate that you're going to take an action, you do it. When you decide on a course of action, you communicate it.

Next is the course itself, the navigating.

You CAN do this.

CHAPTER 12

CAN LEADERSHIP · NAVIGATE

Author's Note: I've already alluded to the course of action or the goal. Navigating is the goal, the vision, the legacy you are working toward. Remember, these three Pillars of Leadership work together for you to lead yourself (and others). Take one away and the other two suffer. You CAN Lead yourself. Then you'll FLY: First Lead Yourself!

**In order to chart any course, you have to
first know where you are.**

When Dan Bornarth was twenty-seven, he joined the Navy. He had an advantage; he was not only older but also had aviation experience. However, as a flight school student, he felt a mile behind the aircraft. It was so different from the civilian flying experience he had learned from his own father.

During one of the flight school phases, Dan was a student in a modified business-class jet, the Cessna Citation T-47A trainer, as a prospective radar intercept officer (RIO).

The U.S. Navy acquired fifteen Cessna T-47A aircraft to train naval flight operators. Modifications included shorter wings and tactical dual-purpose air-to-air and air-to-ground radar.

The T-47A trainer had the student RIO in the right seat and a rated pilot in the left seat with an instructor pilot in the jump seat that swings out behind the pilot seats. The students were being graded on mission operations and would take turns in the copilot seat.

This was one of the final phases to become a winged naval flight officer (NFO) in U.S. Naval Flight Officer Training. The pilot, Bob, was a civilian former F-4 Phantom Fighter Pilot. Dan described Bob, a Vietnam Veteran, as the "John Wayne of the skies." Their mission was to train in specialized radar intercept skills and airways navigation during a cross-country flight from Pensacola, Florida to Alameda, California.

112

Roger flew the first leg of the flight to California and after a refueling stop his partner Dan strapped into the right seat and prepared for his evaluation. Randy, a P-3C Orion NFO and instructor pilot, climbed into the jump seat with a hot cup of coffee in his hand.

In this aircraft, the pilots could isolate the intercom to specific seats. "John Wayne," aka Bob, hot mic-ed a communication just to Dan. "Can you believe this? He's got a cup of coffee in our mighty orange and white tactical jet aircraft without a lid. Not smart." Bob and Dan knew the maneuverability and power that their naval aircraft had and what it could do.

Bob suggested to Dan that he switch over to the tower and ask for an unrestricted climb at takeoff. The tower cleared the aircraft for an unrestricted climb not to exceed 5,000 feet above ground level, so Bob taxied the aircraft into position and readied for takeoff. The unrestricted climb follows a low–transition wind over the wings with just enough altitude to enter ground effect and lift the landing gear while still over the runway. At the end of the runway, Bob pulled back hard to a hard vertical climb. Randy was holding his coffee cup out in front of him, chasing the movements of the aircraft to prevent it from spilling.

Then, as the aircraft approached 4,800 feet above ground level, Bob bumped the nose to stop the climb faster and achieve a zero-gravity effect. As Dan watched out of his peripheral vision, Randy's coffee rose out of his cup and started floating, the oily brown liquid four inches in front of Randy's face.

Bob pulled back on the yoke, putting G-forces back into the airframe and stopping the zero-gravity effect. The coffee followed

the movement of the airplane and splashed straight back on Randy's face and flight suit shoulders.

Even as students, Roger, who was watching from the back, and Dan both knew this was a funny teachable moment. And if Randy had been more aware of the situation (flying with an F-4 jet pilot on board) and anticipating any possible scenario, he would have at least brought his coffee on board with a lid. (I'm sure he did from then on.)

Dan went on to become an instructor pilot himself. Once he was talking with a student while teaching low-level navigation on a flight from Pensacola, FL, to Chattanooga, TN. The course was set, and there was a five-mile limit to each side of the center line of the course. Although that course was new to the student, Dan had flown it many times and was familiar with the landmarks and visual cues en route. Dan knew the student was heading off course. The student was earnest and trying too hard, overthinking it and getting in his own way.

"So where are we?" Dan asked over the radio.

"You mean right now, Sir?"

Dan turned his head to the side away from the student and tried not to laugh. Then he coached the student as he worked to navigate back on course.

Do you know where you ARE in your life? The first step in charting your course is knowing where you are currently. Most of us don't even consider or look at this step. We're so focused on the

goal, our end destination, that we forget to assess if we're prepared for the journey.

You've already read multiple stories in this book about the pilots and the training and the process to get to training. We all had one thing in common: we started from where we were. There is no other place you can start from. So evaluate your starting place.

The second part is knowing where you want to go. That part seems easier, right? Most of us give more thought to that. A vision board (a visual collage of things you want to come true in your life) is a great tool. What are your goals for your life, business, and family? Get specific. Your brain likes specificity, which is why creating a vision board is so powerful.

Many of us reach a point in our life when we realize that we have simply been traveling on autopilot. This may be the result of a traumatic event that may not have been dealt with in the appropriate manner or for a number of different reasons, but one thing is for sure: going through life on autopilot is not a healthy and productive way to live.

I have put together a list of ways in which you can tell if you are living life on autopilot:

> • **You feel trapped**. In many cases, you have a vision of where you will be in the next five years. In some cases, that may be a good thing, but in others, it may leave you feeling trapped by your future. If you feel trapped by what your future holds, it may be time for you to wake up and make some changes. Sometimes, what may have felt like the

right decision in the past does not feel right for the place that you are right now.

• **You followed the dreams of others**. One of the worst decisions you can possibly make is to live the life that someone else planned. Trying to fulfill someone else's dreams will only leave you feeling unfulfilled. If you realize that you have been living this way on autopilot, it is time for you take control and do something that will make you happy.

• **You haven't taken time to explore**. This happens to many people who have gone straight from school to work or college. If you are one of them, you may feel like you are on autopilot because you didn't allow yourself time to adjust to the big change. Many experts recommend that if you find yourself in this situation, that you take yourself off autopilot and take some time to breathe.

Living on autopilot is not a fulfilling way to live. The sooner that you notice you are acting on autopilot, the easier it will be for you to make the necessary changes and begin living the life you have always wanted.

Then there are those times when you are lost along the way. These are the times when you can't see your way out of the forest because all you see are the trees around you, and you don't know which way to go. You might feel stuck. Know one thing: it happens to ALL OF US! You are not alone in this, although that is of little consolation when you are in the muck of it.

In the helicopter, when we would get lost, the procedure was to go back to our last known point so we would know where we were. In order to do that, we would climb in altitude to get a better perspective, to be able to see all the landmarks to make our way.

You might have to climb to a higher altitude in your life. You might have to step away and outside from what you are doing. You might have to make some quiet space and time for thinking things through to shift your awareness.

You only get ONE life. You only get one chance at TODAY. This is it.

Right now, put your hand, doesn't matter which one, up toward your face and put your middle finger on the tip of your nose. Hold it there.

Feel that warm breath against the palm of your hand? You're breathing! It means you have another chance to do something AMAZING with today. Don't wait until tomorrow. Start right now. Remember, there is no autopilot in life; this life IS your MISSION. You have to take action to accomplish it.

Your life is your mission. It's up to you to make the decision to change it. It's up to you to lead yourself through that change to make it happen.

Do you feel like a navigator yet?

Communicate, aviate (take action), and navigate your life. You CAN lead yourself through it.

*Go to **pilotmethod.com/goal-setting-sheets** to download a
complimentary goal-setting guide to help you with your
long-term and short-term goals.*

CHAPTER 13

SEE A NEED LEAD

I was stationed at Fort Drum, New York, during the great 1998 North American ice storm. One hundred and fifteen hours of freezing rain fell on upstate New York, Vermont, New Hampshire, Maine, and large sections of Canada. Over five million people were without power, some of them for months. The ice accumulated so thick the salt wouldn't melt it and the snowplows couldn't get through it to break it up. The area was impassable. We at Fort Drum had buried our power lines, making the base fully operational in the disaster. Since we knew this once-in-a-century-type storm was coming, our aircraft had been stored in the hangers to protect them from the snow and ice.

My unit got the call from the New York Governor's office: "We need two aircraft, Black Hawks, to fly down to Albany to transport the governor, FEMA, the congressman, and the congresswoman to see their constituents and assess the damage."

I received the call. Because I was a single parent, I arranged childcare for my daughter before heading out on the icy roads to the flight line to start planning the mission.

It was going to be a tricky mission. It was cloudy. Clouds are made of water, and it was below freezing. Flying a helicopter in icing was not my favorite flight mode. The anti-icing systems are delicate and complex and if any one system fails, it puts the aircraft and crew in jeopardy.

To get to Albany, we'd be flying in the clouds in icing in instrument mode for the first forty-five minutes of flight, making for a tricky flight plan. The last half of the flight we'd be south of the cloud line caused by the air moving from west to east over the Great Lakes and flying visually (visual flight rules).

The pilot in command was Chief Warrant Officer 2 Deke, and although he and I were the same rank, Deke had attained his pilot in command (PIC) status and I had not. As PIC, he could choose the seat he wanted, and he chose the left seat, leaving the right seat for me. In the back was a lieutenant colonel (LTC) from our brigade operations. The brigade is four levels up the chain of command from our platoon level (platoon, company, battalion, brigade), and we didn't know him. The LTC was to be the liaison between the Governor's office and the Black Hawk crews.

Deke and I filed the flight plan, taking care of all the details for the flight and mission. With the Black Hawk preflighted, our last step was to pull the aircraft out of the warm hangar and out on the barren icy tarmac. Not another aircraft was in sight. The maintenance support hangar was full of Black Hawks with the smaller OH-58D Kiowa Scouts scattered in between, protecting the expensive aircraft from potential damage due to the icing.

It was eerie, standing in the cold wind and hearing the unusual silence of the airfield, the thick ice crunching underneath our

flyers' boots as the crew wing-walked alongside the Black Hawk under each rotor blade to ensure clearance to get the helicopter out of the hangar to a safe distance for run-up.

Strapped on, started up, ready to go, the LTC was in the back, I was on the controls, and all systems were at full operational power, including the anti-icing systems. Deke was handling the communications. He got us cleared for takeoff. We hovered up and then forward, gaining speed and altitude until the windshields were completely white with the clouds, and we were immersed in the pearly white swirls of the skies. Immediately switching over to the instrument mode, I followed air traffic control's instructions in heading and altitude and smoothly transitioned the aircraft to comply.

The flight progressed normally. At about twenty minutes in, as we settled into the flight, checking fuel consumption, scanning our instruments, and maintaining alertness, we heard:

"WAH, WAH, WAH."

OH SHHHHOOOOT! The master caution alarm was blaring and blinking red. Instantly at a higher state of alertness, I monitored the controls. Did I feel anything different? Often with an emergency, you'll feel a shake, a shudder, or a hard push or jerk on the controls—something that indicates what is wrong. *Is it hydraulic? Is it electrical? Is it one of the many complex systems the Black Hawk has?*

Something was wrong, but I didn't feel anything unusual with the controls. We were in icing, in the clouds. I was communicating to Deke that the controls felt normal as I aviated, maintaining

121

aircraft control. I looked over at Deke, and he was panicking, flipping through the pages on the checklist frantically. He was muttering,

"Oh my God, oh my God, oh my God, oh my God..."

"Deke, we need to find what caused the alarm!" I said.

In a Black Hawk, there is almost four feet of instrument panel with a lower console of radios and navigation equipment and a center upper panel with power levers, switches, and fire control. Then there are panels of circuit breakers behind each pilot's head. There is a lot to check and scan.

I saw that the little rectangular lights on the RPM engine #2 gauge were fluctuating low to high, up and down. That was not good! My brain went ice-cold with the emergency.

I started thinking through the system. When you are in a car, can you hear a difference in the engine between gunning the gas and coasting or braking? There is a difference in the sound and the power. The same is true in a Black Hawk.

If you've ever been around helicopters or jet planes, you probably know they are LOUD. I heard engine #2 right over my head. It was roaring at a steady rate, and immediately I knew from my emergency procedures that the raw data was good, but the computer chip that puts the information into the gauge was malfunctioning. If it were a true oscillation of engine power, the other engine would also be oscillating up and down, chasing and compensating for the malfunctioning engine. Since only engine #2 was fluctuating, it meant that the power was stable.

In a flash, I knew it was a signal data converter chip malfunction.

"Deke, it's the signal data converter. It's a chip malfunction. We're okay," I said.

"No, no, no!" he shouted. "Oscillating RPM; I need to pull that engine back." The emergency procedure in the checklist for an oscillating engine reads:

"The suggested pilot corrective action is to pull back the ENG POWER CONT lever of the suspected engine until oscillation stops."

However, we were in icing, in the clouds, and I knew that the complex anti-icing and de-icing systems rely on a combination of electrical and engine air and heated oil that must be maintained for the anti-icing to work.

This was all racing through my thinking with complete clarity, at a speed that was surprising. All the time I had spent studying the operator's manual clicked into place.

I tried to reason with him. "Deke, NO. I'm maintaining aircraft control, altitude, and airspeed. The engine sounds normal." Only seconds had passed since the emergency alarm had sounded.

Deke, with his eyes wide and panic in his voice, argued, "No, the emergency procedure says!" He reached up to put his hand on the throttle for engine #2.

What would you do? What do you do when someone is in a position of authority (like the pilot in command), and he or she is going to do something that is wrong, something that would have a negative consequence, something that would put your life (and the lives of others) at risk?

When I tell this story in my keynote speeches, I hear, "I'd hit him." But my hands were on the controls. I was flying the aircraft without an autopilot feature in an emergency situation. Would you take your hands off the controls?

I yelled into the intercom, "Do NOT TOUCH that throttle, Deke! If you want to wait until we are out of this icing and in a safer mode of flight, be my guest. I can fly this aircraft on one engine then. You WILL NOT pull that throttle back while I am flying this aircraft. Look it up in the book."

I was not going to put the aircraft and my crew at risk and leave my daughter without a mother. NOT HAPPENING. We didn't have iPads or tablets back then. The "book" was the operator's manual that was over 600 pages and four inches thick. It was difficult to flip through while in the cockpit, as space was limited. Deke's hand slid off the throttle; his eyes were wide as he stared at me.

I looked over at him. "Go on. Look it up in the book!" I ordered.

I could see his lips moving as he muttered under his breath. He reached behind the seat and pulled out the binder and started flipping pages. I continued to fly. All systems responded normally, and all indicators were normal except for the gauge of engine #2, which continued to slide up and down. Out of the corner of my eye, I saw Deke still flipping pages. We flew out of the clouds, out of the icing, and I breathed a sigh of relief and flexed my hand, which was sweaty inside my glove.

We continued visually east toward Albany, and I saw Deke put the operator's manual back into place. I waited to see what he would say. Oh, he had maintained communication with the Air Traffic Control Center, but he hadn't said much to me since. As we conducted our before-landing checks and maneuvered into final approach at Albany's airport, Deke clicked on the intercom and said, "Crew Chief, please write up this aircraft for a signal data converter chip malfunction."

Good idea! I kept that to myself. We continued into landing and, after some calls, found the part that was needed. Some maintenance management was required. It took a couple of days to get the part delivered and installed and the aircraft back to operational, but we were finally good to go.

The lieutenant colonel came up to me and said, "Chief Mac, we have a mission tomorrow. You're going to go here and here and here…"

I pulled out my handy, dandy notebook and started writing down the details. "Yes, Sir. We'll take care of it, Sir!" And I turned and took the notebook to Deke, the pilot in command, to plan the mission. Although we prep and plan, not all of these missions get

off the ground due to weather or changes. And the LTC kept coming up to me with all the updates. This happened again and again.

At the end of the week, the LTC said, "Chief Mac, in my office."

"Yes, Sir."

"Why didn't you tell me you were not the pilot in command?"

Was he mad? I couldn't tell. "Sir, I didn't know that you didn't know."

"Chief, I know you don't know this, but before I flew a desk, I flew Black Hawks, too. And I was plugged into the radios on the flight down. So I knew what was going on. If you hadn't stopped him when you did, I was about to unstrap from my seat, climb over the crew chief, and stop him myself. It's a good thing you did."

All I could think of at the time was, Oh, thank goodness I'm not getting court-martialed for busting my chain of command!

What I learned from that was a life lesson that never leaves me. I was not in a position of authority on that flight. I didn't have it by rank or position. I was low on the chain of command. Yet I had a responsibility to step up to prevent what I knew to be wrong.

Don't wait to be asked.
Don't wait to get promoted.
Don't wait for a nomination.
Don't wait to be elected.

126

Don't wait for someone else to do it first!

You have the ability, the capability, and a responsibility to lead from where you are right NOW.

When you see a need, LEAD from where you ARE!

That's how you lead yourself. And what happens when you lead yourself is that people start following you.

The P.I.L.O.T. Method

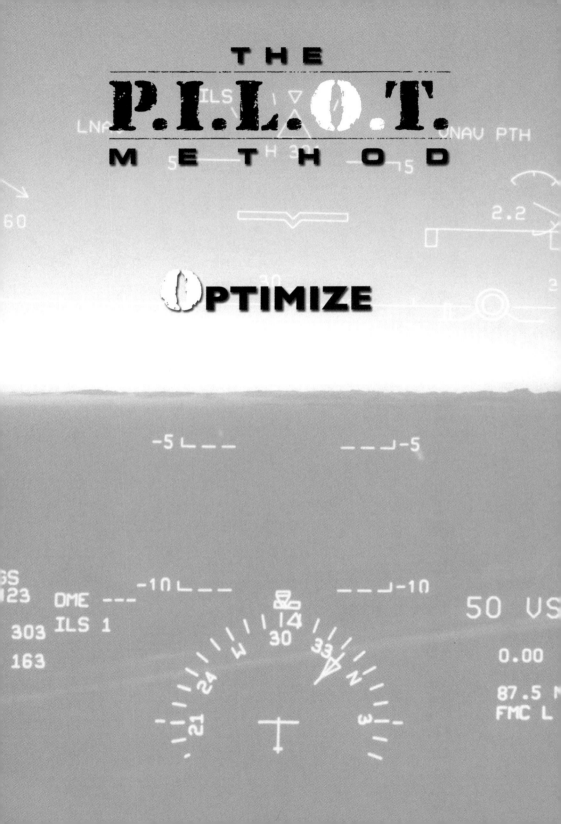

The P.I.L.O.T. Method

CHAPTER 14

OPTIMAL PERFORMANCE

When I went to that first duty assignment at Fort Drum, New York, I was in for a rude awakening.

In flight school training, the advanced aircraft transition course after that, and the Warrant Officer Basic Course, we all worked long days!

We had:

Physical training early every morning
Quick hygiene time
Classes Quick lunch
Flight line training Study group

Then the schedule would flip, and I would have flight line training starting early in the morning, followed by a quick lunch. After lunch were classes, then physical fitness at the end of the day, and then study group.

While the rest of the flight school students went to their homes to sleep or went out for a few beers, I would go pick up my daughter from child care in a service member's home. Then I would spend time with my not quite one-year-old baby. I wasn't getting much sleep.

When I moved to upstate New York, completed my in processing, and set up my orientation with CW3 Santos, I was surprised when he explained that this was now the real world, and he asked me if I was familiar with "crew rest."

From flight school, the primary concern for crew rest was no alcohol for twelve hours before flying. "Twelve hours bottle to throttle" it was called.

I learned about peak performance. I've heard a lot about "peak" performance, "peak" potential, "peak" this or that. When there is a peak though, there is a valley. When there is a high, there is a low. When there is a crest, there is a crash. A high can't be sustained. I learned about achieving an optimal performance: a higher level that is supportable, sustainable, and maintainable.

As I consciously lived my life optimally, I could see the difference. With peak performance and the highs and lows, the average was often, well, average with flashes of both brilliance and mediocrity.

Living your life optimally takes effort. It requires focus and full-on commitment.

It starts with the one thing that most of us don't do well: taking care of ourselves.

132

The programming starts with our mothers. We see our mothers in their nurturing roles taking care of us as children. Our mothers sacrifice, eat cold food as they are last to sit at the table, and do without so their children can have something they didn't have. Most mothers take care of everyone else before taking care of themselves.

Yet, when mom is sick, is she able to take care of anyone else? Does anything get done the way mom would do it? Probably not.

You have a responsibility to take care of yourself because if you don't take care of yourself, who will take care of you? Maybe you still have a parent or parents. Thank them every day because not everyone does. Maybe you have a spouse or partner who takes care of you. Appreciate him or her every day, as so many do not. But most of us don't have someone who can step in and step up to take care of us.

So we need to take care of ourselves.

What do I mean by take care of yourself? You need to take care of yourself in the following ways:

> • **Physically**. This is the ONLY body you get. You can pierce it, tattoo it, and alter it with plastic surgery or cosmetic procedures. But this is it. You can't change that. Sure, it would be nice if we could upgrade or trade it in, but it doesn't work like that, does it? So eat right, exercise, and get sleep. If you don't CHOOSE to nourish your body, strengthen your body, and rest your body so you are at an optimal performance level, who will?

It starts with you; it stops with you. No excuses, no waiting until tomorrow. Make YOU a priority. Put YOU time on a calendar and make it unbreakable time. If you make it a "when I get to it" item, you won't get to it!

Today is all you get. Be kind to your body and treat yourself well. When you treat yourself with respect, others are more likely to follow. Pilots are especially conscious of physical limitations and the need to keep their bodies in top shape; their flight status counts on the results of an annual physical.

> • **Emotionally**. Remember that emotional instability is draining. Pilots have to learn to compartmentalize their emotions. There is no room for them in the aircraft. Everything that happens before the flight is locked in a room in your mind. It has to be so you can focus on what you're doing right now.

Be kind to yourself. Don't beat yourself up when you make mistakes. Step back from mistakes and look objectively at them and ask yourself:

"What can I learn from that?"

"How can I prevent this from happening again?"

"What can I do differently?

Then move on. We get stuck when we can't let go of things that are not serving us. Learn from them and let go. Forgive yourself.

Forgive others. When we hold on to grudges, that negativity festers and burns in us. It hurts us and affects our capacity to love and live life as well as our willingness to be vulnerable and feel. Forgiving others can give you peace.

Is it easy? Not always. It wasn't easy for me to forgive the pilot who stalked me and was physically abusive to me in my workplace. But I wasn't willing to continue to give him power over my emotions. I wasn't willing to keep the negative energy of being unforgiving.

• **Intellectually**. John C. Maxwell, the best-selling leadership expert, says:

"Leaders are lifelong learners."

And it's true. If you want to lead yourself in life, you will want to continue to grow and learn. Pilots constantly study to ensure they stay sharp mentally on their system limitations and their emergency procedures (chapters five and nine). It's more than a necessity though; it's a quiet urge to be better, to do more, to not settle for less than your personal best.

I call it being your "best-est." I'm creating that word right here in this book for you. In order to be your "best-est," you have to study those who have walked in the shoes before you.

For pilots, this means following the flight instructor and reading history of aviation, aerodynamics, and engineering. I've translated this intellectual propensity into my business by having mentors who are where I strive to be, by reading books like this one, and by pushing my comfort zone so far and so hard that I no

longer even know where it is! I've gotten comfortable with that discomfort.

> • **Spiritually**. Whatever your source is, stay connected to that. It will give you peace during difficult times. When I was interviewing pilots for this book, several mentioned their faith in their source and how that got them through layoffs, near crashes, and deployments.

For me, as a Christian, it was surrendering to God during the abuse I mentioned earlier. I thought I was going to die. I knew that it could happen and completely surrendered my life to God's love. I thought that maybe God needed me as His copilot more than I was needed on earth. This was an uncomfortable thought, as I was still a single parent to my daughter. If I didn't have my faith through that, the what-if from being stalked and never knowing when an attack would come might have broken me. It certainly felt like it was more than I could bear.

I know that the reason I went through that is so that I can help people who have gone through abuse to know they aren't alone. I was twenty-seven years old and one of some four hundred female helicopter pilots in the WORLD at that point (as I was told at the end of flight school). I was physically strong.

Yet I was still physically, verbally, and emotionally abused. It can happen to anyone, male or female.

You can choose to take care of you and make yourself a priority in your life. That's how you live an optimal life. There are no shortcuts. It takes work, discipline, and the willpower to be willing to do that work—even when it's a sacrifice.

CHAPTER 15

IT TAKES A TEAM

Another way to optimize your life is to carefully choose whom you spend your time with as you build a team around you. As an aviator at that first unit, I learned the concept of crew and how important it is to build your team, choosing carefully who will be in your crew.

In the Army, as well as in aviation in general, there are many people that make the flight missions happen:

- The weather team
- The operations for mission assignments
- The tower operations for filing the flight plans
- The company scheduler who determines which pilots will fly the missions by creating the flight schedule
- The maintenance support unit
- The refueling crew (We don't get anywhere without fuel!)
- The crew chiefs who fly with the aircraft and perform the daily maintenance on the aircraft
- The units we supported and flew missions for (customers)

- The pilots, of course

Carol, a commercial airline pilot with a major carrier, describes the team that supports the pilots as well as providing friendly, reliable, and low-cost air travel:

The airline takes care of details, filing the flight plan, fueling, providing weather packets, notices to airman (NOTAMs), maintenance, etc. The pilots preflight, walk around the aircraft, prepare the cockpit, review the flight plan (known as the release), review the weather, and decide if more fuel needs to be brought on.

If we have to go into a holding pattern because of weather at a destination, we plan accordingly. We might have to hold for so many minutes and either fly to an alternate to refuel or continue to the airport, but still have fuel to execute a missed approach and fly to an alternate. We have to plan ahead, have contingencies, so we don't put ourselves in a low-fuel state, which puts the passengers at risk. Safety is the priority that pilots and the team of support staff work toward on every flight.

As a young pilot, I watched and I learned. I took the crappy "rookie" jobs, like stocking the platoon refrigerator with drinks, seriously, did them well, and paid attention. What I saw was that the crew chiefs had pilots they liked and pilots they definitely did not like. The unlikeable pilots were the ones who left garbage on the aircraft or, worse, flew troops and would purposely fly rough, inevitably resulting in someone losing his or her breakfast on board. And who had to clean that up?

138

The crew chiefs...

If the crew chiefs liked you, they took care of you when you had a mission. They could position your seat for you and work with the platoon sergeant to make sure your assigned helicopter was in the hangar for preflight so you weren't outside in the frigid cold opening hatches and checking systems. If the crew chief didn't like you, you'd be freezing your legs off while preflighting all around and on top of the helicopter. Worse, the crew chief would find something wrong on the helicopter you were assigned for a training mission—not a real mission—and keep the aircraft from flying that day. Either another aircraft would be assigned, which would be a lot of duplicate work because all the paperwork would have to be revised as well as the preflight, causing a delay or, worse, making it so the "un-liked" pilot won't get to fly at all! The crew chiefs, despite being the lower-ranking part of the flight crew, actually held a lot of power. They literally could scrub and reduce your flight time. I saw this happen over and over to pilots who were inconsiderate.

Because of this, I made it a mission to take care of the crew chiefs in my platoon. I found out their favorite foods, candy, and desserts and would bring something to work every Monday to "share." When we had to do field training for days at a time in the field, I kept a stash of my crew chiefs' favorite candy bars. It was a small thing in cost but greatly appreciated after several days of eating the prepackaged, preservative-filled "Meals Ready to Eat" (MREs).

Once they saw this treatment wasn't just a suck-up and that I maintained it and was genuine in my appreciation, they took care of me as well. They took care of more than the aircraft. During

those field exercises when the tent was set up, the crew chiefs would reserve a corner for me, as I was the only female out there, and without asking me, they would hang a cord across the beams of the tent and laid a plastic camouflage poncho over it so I had some privacy.

It wasn't because of my rank. It wasn't because I was a pilot. It was because I treated them right FIRST. I took the initiative and went out of my way to show my crew chiefs I noticed them. I "SAW" them, as in the movie Avatar. I paid attention to how much work it took to keep up the helicopters and appreciated it. I saw the people behind the job. I wasn't demanding. I didn't call attention to the fact that I was the lone woman or higher-ranking officer.

What if we do this with everyone who has a role in our lives, our business, our careers? Do you pay attention to the cleaning crew at your school or job? Do you ever say "Thank you"? Or are you only sharing your attention with the ones that you want something from? People NOTICE that!

My father taught me, "Always be nice. Everyone is worthy of your respect, and you never know who might be your boss, in a hiring position, or your customer in the future."

I've taught my own daughter (that infant is now grown) to look for this while dating, to watch how a boy, a prospective suitor, treats his mother, his sister, and the waitress at a restaurant. This tells you a lot about people. Is it all about THEM, or are they willing to share their attention, personality, and appreciation with people in all positions?

How would you measure up if you were being assessed? Building your team applies to your own life this way and also to how you choose the people who become your friends.

"You are the average of the five people you spend the most time with."
~Jim Rohn

We automatically gravitate toward two kinds of people: those like us or those who are the far opposite from us. The choice we make as to who our closest friends are and how much time we spend with those people impacts us much more than we realize.

If your friends are negative, if your friends make you feel bad about yourself, if your friends tear you down to build themselves up... you might consider getting new friends.

A friend is someone who builds you up. A friend is someone who brightens your day, who is there for you. Be a good friend back to your friends. Choose to be around positive people!

And here's the kicker: you need to be positive too, so they want to be around you!

The P.I.L.O.T. Method

CHAPTER 16

ATTITUDE

Yes, I'm going there. I already shared with you about my negative attitude in high school.

My second favorite quote is:

"Your attitude, not your aptitude,
will determine your altitude."
~Zig Ziglar

Zig was right. It's not about smarts. It's about your "CAN do"and "Want to."

I was retired from the Army with a career-ending medical condition that will never let me fly again. EVER. I am a permanently grounded pilot. It would have been easy to fall into a pity party for myself. My entire future as I had it planned was gone with one medical diagnosis: Meniere's disease, an inner ear dysfunction causing hearing loss, pain, vertigo, and tinnitus. My flight career was over. No more soaring. No possibility for becoming a commercial airline pilot. And, at the same time, my ex-husband, the starter husband, was suing me for custody.

I had so many negative things going on in my life. It would have been easy to focus on that negative.

Consider all the negatives:

- Lost flight status
- Medical condition reported to the FAA
- Never able to fly again, ever
- Lost my job with the military
- SUED for custody
- No job
- No car
- No house or apartment

I could have VERY easily gone into despair and made it about the negatives in my life. After all, I was planning on becoming an airline pilot after my Army contract was up, and I had just lost my career, my future plans, and my health.

Instead, I CHOSE to focus on ANYTHING that was positive and what I could be grateful for:

- I had other training in the military that translated to the job market.
- There was a new job posting website called "Monster.com," and I had a job interview lined up for the second day I would be home.
- I was going home to Texas where I would get to see my family after not being home for two years.
- I was thirty years old and about to start drawing military retirement benefits.
- My health could have been worse. I still had the use of my arms and legs, my eyesight, and partial hearing.

- The pilot training actually helped me cope with my disease.

I could overcome the vertigo through willpower, ignoring it and paying attention to the visual cues around me, much like flying in instrument mode, my favorite flight mode.

- I had my five-year-old daughter to think of.

At the time, I didn't consciously realize what I was doing. I was searching for the positives in my life. I believed that there had to be something, anything, I could focus on to keep my attitude up. It was a choice to be positive in a time that was…not.

I remember my mother calling me in Germany in tears about me losing my flight career and my job at the same time. And I said to her, "It'll be *okay*."

"But…"

"*I'll be okay*." And I firmly believed it. If I believed I would be okay, there was no option for me to not be okay.

Have you ever been at that crossroads in your life—a time when you were in a negative cycle? You are not alone. What makes the difference is being proactive in LEADING yourself OUT OF IT!

So how do you do that? You start by boosting your belief that you have the potential to be positive. During the difficult times, I found myself standing in front of my mirror talking to myself.

"You can do this."
"You'll get through this."
"You will come out thriving."

Those phrases eventually morphed into the stronger "I AM" statements. I've been using these I AM statements for more than twenty years now to strengthen myself.

Now I do these I AM statements every morning and night in front of the mirror while I brush my teeth—first inside my head and then again out loud when I'm done with the toothbrush!

"I am powerful."
"I am confident."
"I am smart."
"I am great at..."

Over and over, these words change based on what I need to accomplish in my day! I prepare myself for my day because if I don't do this and boost my beliefs, potential, and attitude to prepare me for the day ahead, who will?

> To help you start using "I AM" exercises, download Elizabeth's I AM handout at:
>
> pilotmethod.com/I-AM-handout
>
> And in the comments, share your favorite or a new I AM statement.

No one! We have to boost our attitude and ourselves. We are responsible for our attitudes, our moods, and how we show up in the world. We need to be proactive in our attitude.

Have you ever found yourself saying any of the following?

"I'll do it tomorrow."
"It really doesn't need to be done right now."
"It's not my problem."
"It's not in my job description." (I really don't like to hear this one!)

Sure you have. I am fairly certain everyone has said at least one of those statements at some point in your life. Does that make you a non-proactive person? If those types of statements come out of your mouth or cross your mind on a regular basis—possibly!

The only way to solve a problem is to find some sort of resolution, and in order to do that, you have to be proactive and look at the problem. The more positive your attitude is when looking at the problem for a possible resolution, the better chance you'll have for a favorable outcome. Now, again, problems only appear big in relation to how positive your outlook is. The more positive you are, the smaller the problem will appear. The more negative you are, the bigger and likely insurmountable the problem will appear.

Challenges in your life can be an opportunity for growth, especially if you are proactive with a positive attitude. You gain strength with each issue you overcome, and what once may have been a huge problem becomes conquerable.

A positive attitude will allow you to overcome challenges, give you a sense of accomplishment, and lead to positive self-esteem which, in turn, helps you to feel good about your own abilities and capacities.

A positive attitude is what helps us grow, mature, and attract even more positivity in our lives. Success is not a birthright; it is something gained through strategy and having a positive self-image and self-esteem. Does this mean we never question ourselves? No, but it does mean that when we do question ourselves, we also remember our strengths and build upon what we know we are great at. And everybody is great at something.

Every day is a choice. Are you going to be positive? That choice has an impact on everything else you do.

INTEGRITY

Have you ever been caught in a lie? Feels bad, doesn't it? Which feels worse: the embarrassment and disgrace of getting caught or the embarrassment and disgrace of having lied in the first place?

As kids, most of us learn that honesty is the best policy. I did. I painfully remember two childhood memories of doing something dishonest and getting caught. Those memories are embedded into my brain as something not to do, and therefore, as an adult, I choose to be honest in everything I do. So yes, that means when the cashier at the store gives me change for a twenty-dollar bill when I gave her a ten-dollar bill, I give the difference back. Integrity means doing the right thing even when no one is looking.

During the last weeks of Warrant Officer Candidate School (WOCS), I damaged my integrity. I misrepresented myself. Because of my ability to lead myself, despite having much less experience than many of the other candidates in school, I was chosen to be the candidate executive officer (XO). We had a candidate commander and a candidate first sergeant. For the last two weeks of the six-week cycle, in addition to our regular duties, we were "in

charge" of leading the other two "younger" classes. There was a lot to do, and we had permission to stay up one hour later than everyone else to get things done (and get less sleep, too).

I was tasked with speaking to our TAC officer and receiving permission to perform these duties. Have you ever thought about something so much, visualizing how you wanted to handle the conversation and what the outcome was, that you FELT like you had already had the conversation? I did in this instance, and although I had intended to have it completed, it was not. However, when the candidate commander asked me if it was complete, I said it was.

Within the span of that day, the lie unraveled. He saw the TAC officer before I had a chance to, and you can guess how that conversation went. It wasn't pretty. I had messed up, and now I was embarrassed. Worse, I had diminished my credibility.

When the candidate commander confronted me that night at our evening meeting, it was ugly. I had made a mistake. All I could do was take responsibility, yet it wasn't enough.

As he put it, "Now every time I ask you if something is done, I'm going to wonder if it really is. You've broken that trust that is your word, and I'm not sure if the ten days we have left in the course is enough to build that trust back up."

That was almost twenty years ago and yet I can remember every word! I never wanted to feel that way again. I was only twenty-three years old and in a position of responsibility that many others struggled with.

Did I go in with the attitude of "I'm young, so I can screw it up?" No! When I made that mistake, did I make excuses for myself, such as "I'm young; I'm still learning?" No! I took responsibility for my actions, learned from my mistake, and vowed to never do that again. And I still carry the weight of my actions.

Integrity is a character trait that some carry heavily and others, well, not so much.

When we live with a strong conviction to integrity, we live honest lives and are true to our word and actions. It is an active choice we make each morning when we wake. We carry this with us throughout our day and make no exceptions. By doing so, we make it easier for others to trust and depend on us and, in reality, make our own lives simpler.

We become forthright people who don't ever have to worry about hiding anything. People with integrity hold themselves accountable for their actions or lack thereof. It is like a code of honor.

"Real Integrity is doing the right thing, knowing that nobody's going to know whether you did it or not."
~Oprah Winfrey

Integrity is a personal value. It is something you truly believe in and something you are not willing to compromise. It plays an active role in every decision you make, even when it isn't convenient. It isn't just defined by your work ethic but by everything you do. Your integrity defines you.

151

When you do make a mistake, as we all do from time to time, the difference having integrity makes is owning up to it immediately, accepting the consequences that may come with it, and doing your best to make it right. Having integrity means you embrace your values. Integrity means you're honest, you keep your word, and you act on sound judgment.

Integrity, as well as self-esteem, requires self-awareness. Integrity requires being able to stand up for what is right even when it doesn't win you any popularity points. When you can't stand up for yourself, it is much harder to stand up for others.

Positive self-esteem helps us to feel good about our own abilities and capacities. It is what helps us grow, mature, and attract positivity in our lives.

Solid integrity and a positive attitude are attractive to positive people, enabling them to build that strong team around themselves. Taking care of yourself and feeling healthy makes it easier for you to have a positive attitude.

Following the CAN Leadership principles will allow you to lead yourself in life with more ease. It's all connected with action through implementation when you believe in your potential.

The P.I.L.O.T. Method

CHAPTER 18

FAILURE IS AN OPTION

Tom Martinelli, a former Army aviation officer and aeroscout pilot, was deployed to Saudi Arabia with an attack helicopter battalion during Operations Desert Shield and Desert Storm. The unit saw heavy action as a part of the 3rd Armor Division and VII Corps "Hail Mary" sweep across the desert to engage the Iraqi Republican Guard.

Following the cease-fire, his unit was ordered to a forward position in central Kuwait to support units that occupied the thin line between the peacekeeping Coalition Forces and the remnants of Saddam Hussein's Army. The unit saw little action from the end of February to the end of May 1991 and was ordered to redeploy to its home base in Hanau, Germany, in mid-June.

The unit spent a couple of weeks loading their trucks and other supplies. The last phase was to fly the aircraft from Kuwait to a port in Saudi Arabia so they could be loaded on ships bound for Germany. Only one flight was left—a simple, two-and-a-half-hour journey. They would be back in Germany with their loved ones in less than three days. But for now, there was still work to do, and

155

everyone had to stay focused despite a major case of "get home-itis."

It was a hot, beautiful day, no clouds in the sky, and the mission required a formation flight of three OH-58C Kiowa Warrior helicopters and two UH-60 Black Hawks.

The Kiowa is a single-engine, unarmed reconnaissance and scout helicopter. For combat missions, the helicopter is configured light and carries a crew of two pilots and only essential equipment. Such a configuration is necessary for the aircraft to maximize its ability to maneuver close to the ground in search of enemy forces.

On this mission, there would be no enemy contact, and the helicopter was loaded with extra cargo for the redeployment. Tom was the pilot in command of one of the Kiowas, flying single pilot with a crew chief, specialist in rank and E-4 in pay grade, in the other seat. This was not an uncommon flight crew for peacetime missions.

For the first ninety minutes, the flight was normal. Then the first malfunction occurred: a generator failure. As emergency procedures go, it's a nonemergent one. In fact, the checklist response is "Land as Soon as PRACTIBLE" instead of the more urgent possibility of "Land as Soon as POSSIBLE." The OH-58C can fly without a generator, but the battery would only supply electrical power for approximately twenty minutes. Tom communicated through the radio to the other pilots in the multi-ship formation that he was going radio silent and turned off the battery switch, preserving the energy for critical communications and shut down later in the flight.

A stop was required en route for hot gas, meaning refueling with the engine on and rotor turning. At this point, Tom had to make a decision to shut down the helicopter there and request a recovery team be sent to repair it or continue to the port. The decision was made to continue on, and Tom communicated to the other pilots that he would continue to be radio silent during the remainder of the flight until they reached the port.

If you were going to have an engine failure, most of the Saudi terrain would be ideal for it: flat, sandy, and fairly forgiving. As Tom flew over a rock quarry at a speed of ninety knots, at sixty feet above ground level, with a fifteen-knot tailwind, third in the formation flight order, the N1 first stage of the engine dropped below 95 percent. The emergency procedure for this? Execute an autorotation maneuver, as your only engine is likely to fail.

An autorotation is a maneuver every helicopter pilot trains for over and over and over again. Unlike an airplane that has some glide if power is lost, a helicopter drops like a rock. Because the power train is no longer moving the rotors to create lift, it becomes imperative to create airflow to move the rotors to extend airtime and increase the chances of controlling and surviving the impending crash.

Instantly, Tom knew many things simultaneously (creating a mental "Know It All" list). He knew he was going down. He could turn around and put the nose into the wind, making the aircraft easier to control but also, because there were two Black Hawks flying in formation behind him, possibly putting those aircraft at risk for a mid-air collision. He could go forward with the tailwind and autorotate into the rock quarry, one of the few unforgiving terrains he had crossed. Or he could risk attempting to extend his

glide path, knowing that he would have a harder landing on more favorable terrain.

As Tom recounted this story, he doesn't remember processing any of these decisions. These thoughts were flashed through in fractions of a second to make a decision, simultaneously prioritizing and discarding options in his mind while maintaining aircraft control. He doesn't remember if he locked the specialist's harness or if he told him to through the internal communication system. It was seconds before he would make contact with the ground.

The decision was made to increase forward speed and hold some pitch in the blades to move past the quarry to what looked like a smooth area of sand. Just a few feet from hitting the ground, Tom zeroed out his airspeed, leveled the helicopter, and pulled the collective to increase the pitch to exhaust every bit of energy of the rotor system to create a cushioning effect for a semi-controlled landing.

Despite his best efforts, the landing was less than ideal because the land wasn't level. A small clump of sand clustered around a shard of grass created a three-foot pile, enough instability for the faltering aircraft to list to the right, hit a critical rollover point, and roll onto its right side. One of the aircraft blades struck the ground and snapped with a loud "WHAP" sound. Fortunately, the second rotor blade stopped at the tail instead of coming through the cockpit. The aircraft and the blades came to a stop with the fuselage on its right side. Tom was looking up at the specialist crew chief in the left seat, unharmed above him. The specialist said, "I'm getting out."

Tom answered calmly, "Let's wait until we're done crashing." And he calmly performed an emergency shutdown, recording all of the system indicators on the pad of paper strapped to his leg on the kneeboard. Then some oil leaked onto the hot turbine and began spewing black smoke.

As the smoke smell engulfed the crew inside the cockpit, the specialist panicked and unbuckled his harness. He fell on Tom! Then he proceeded to attempt to climb out of the airframe, jumping onto Tom and bruising his ribs.

Up until this point, to Tom, everything felt normal. Training had kicked in. The standard military procedure in a helicopter accident is to meet at fifty feet in front of the helicopter at the twelve o'clock position. After clearing the fuselage, the specialist ran to the nine o'clock position—and kept running! Tom watched, incredulous, wondering why the specialist was running. It seemed so odd and out of place.

As Tom looked back at the twelve o'clock position, he saw that the other aircraft in the flight had landed, and the crew was making sure the specialist was okay. Tom wasn't surprised; he expected the other crews to be there. Everything was as it should be, except the specialist was still running... through the desert.

Was the mission a failure? The aircraft didn't make it to the destination. The crew walked or, in the specialist's case, RAN from the accident, so the personnel were safe.

Pilots have a saying: "Take-offs are optional. Landings are required." Prior to taking off, there are options: abort, delay, or revise the mission. But once we are in the air, there are few

159

choices. Land or crash-land, but eventually we are coming down. With Apollo 13, Johnson Space Center and NASA said, "Failure is not an option." With the astronauts stuck in space, that was an accurate assessment.

But for the rest of us on the ground, it's not about failing. It's about learning from our mistakes. We make mistakes. You've read a few of mine so far. What makes an impact on our life aren't the mistakes themselves but how we handle them.

If you spend all your time being fearful of making a mistake and trying to stay in your comfort zone, although you may not make a mistake, you also aren't living fully in your potential!

You will also never experience anything new or exciting. Your life will center on experiences that you are comfortable with and that you have undoubtedly encountered numerous times. When you are doing things you have done over and over, rarely will you get a different result.

"Everything amazing happens outside your comfort zone."
~Jennifer Aniston

Decide to stretch that comfort zone. Take one step out of it and then another. Take a risk. Make a change. Be the first. Try something new.

Leading yourself means taking a risk, stretching your abilities further than you thought possible. That is how you lead yourself.

And when, not if, you fail and make a misstep, learn from it and try something different again—and again. *That is tenacity.*

CHAPTER 19

YOUR LIFE IS YOUR MISSION

Dale Edelmann was a charter pilot, and a single pilot type-rated in a King Air 350. It was a flexible position, meaning he could fly in the right seat or the left seat, as the pilot in command or copilot. The charter company was with Raytheon Aircraft Charter and Management out of Northern California. A company owned the airplane, and Raytheon held the charter certificate and conducted all the maintenance. The owner of the airplane paid Raytheon to employee the pilots to run the charter flights.

Dale was in his twenties and had already been flying full-time for eighteen months in this aircraft. He was motivated and knew this aircraft inside and out. He babied the aircraft and took responsibility for its care between maintenance periods.

There was a chief pilot that Dale got along with, although he took a lot of time off. The owner didn't like the inconsistencies of having a fill-in for the chief pilot and fired him. Afterward, Dale was called back in to the hangar to meet the replacement. This replacement, Chief Pilot Bill, was a retired Army helicopter pilot who had flown corporate jets for a while. There was a big age difference between Dale and Bill, as well as a difference in

experience levels. Bill was not current in the aircraft, which meant he needed three takeoffs and three landings with some pattern work to get back up to speed.

As Dale took Chief Pilot Bill up for his first flight after the airplane came out of maintenance, he explained their unwritten policy of "babying" this aircraft and running it easy, meaning the pilots did not push full power if it wasn't needed. The first flight was from Northern California to Carlsbad in Southern California. At this airport, about two-thirds of the way down the runway, there was a high-speed turnoff. Bill came in fast, too fast, and stomped on the brakes to make the high speed turn off.

"Those are new brakes," Dale said mildly.

"Then I'm breaking them in," was Bill's response.

Dale was concerned about the disregard for the aircraft. And as the flight continued, he had reason to be concerned. For the return flight out of Carlsbad, the owner of the aircraft was on board. Bill chose to run up the engines in static power, bringing the throttles up with the brakes on. In a turbo prop like the King Air, the turbine engine runs the propellers. As the airflow increases, it creates a ram air effect, increasing the torque output and the power from the engines. And with that increase in the gauges and a rise in torque, there is a load on the propeller also.

The max torque allowed is 100 percent.

As Bill was running up the engines for takeoff, he pushed them to 101 and then 102 percent in torque.

"Watch torque," Dale said. After takeoff, Dale reminded Bill that they did reduced power takeoffs. Communicating with the chief pilot was part of Dale's job as second in command, and busting a systems limitation like that was a safety issue.

"Incorrect!" barked back Bill. Then he started quizzing Dale on the airframe Dale had exclusively flown for almost two years. "Incorrect! Look it up!"

Dale started questioning himself, even though the airplane was still in a precarious flight mode, 3,000 feet above the ocean. Dale pulled out the pilot's operator manual from the left seat. With familiarity, Dale turned right to the correct page and read to Bill.

"Max torque 100%. Max continuous torque 100%." Blustering, Bill responded, "In my experience..."

Dale interrupted, "Limitations do not change based on experience." It was a dangerous situation. Pilots are notoriously cocky and self-absorbed; they have to lead themselves and their flight crew, but Bill was well beyond what was normal. To Dale, it wasn't about being RIGHT; it was about being safe.

Bill constantly quizzed Dale, being disapproving and dismissive of anything he did.

Dale did not want to quit his job, and yet he wanted to quit his job badly! He did not want to work with Bill one more day. Dale had choices. Three different times over the next year, he almost quit. He stayed mainly because of his wife, a house payment, and the bills.

Dale knew it wouldn't take long for Bill to leave. Bill wasn't a good fit in the company culture. It was only a matter of time. What Dale learned was to keep himself in a good light with the company. In his own words, he "stayed polite." He chose to meet company expectations and build better relationships. In fact, because Bill was so demanding, the maintenance staff hated him, and Dale would go behind him and put out the fires and smooth things over with the support staff. Dale actually built stronger relationships with the support staff because of the contrast.

Dale knew that, in order to keep from blowing up or losing his temper, he had to "throttle it back." There he was, in his twenties, an aggressive guy, and his prideful nature was to put Bill in his place. But Dale looked at the situation and made the DECISION to suck it up. He had to maintain composure, because he had more riding on this than Bill did. So he swallowed his pride, and sure enough, about a year later, Bill quit to pursue a nonflying career.

It would have been easy to quit. In fact, it would have been EASIER on Dale to quit. Instead, he stuck with it. Dealing with a difficult person like Bill may be one of the hardest things you will encounter in your life.

Acting out emotionally can be detrimental to your potential, your present, and your future. It requires a decision and discipline to stop yourself from reacting emotionally in these situations that will come your way. Put your reaction into perspective.

Stop and think: Is this reaction going to help me or hurt me?

As you make that determination about your reaction, ask yourself: "Does this help me or hurt me?" This thinking pulls you

164

out of an emotional response and into a logical one. To be sure you're thinking logically, ask yourself: "Will this make a difference in five years? Will this make a difference in ten years? Is this something I'm willing to take a stand for, with potentially negative results?"

In my own case, even during the ice storm as I was doing the right thing and standing up to the pilot in command in the emergency procedure, there was still a part of me that wondered, Will I get in trouble for this? I did what I did because I was willing to accept the responsibility for my actions.

It was a calculated risk.

When thinking through what the possible outcomes could be, consider that:

"If I do this, this could happen."

"If I do that, that could happen."

"If I don't do this, this could happen."

Stop! Think! Take the time to let anger and emotions fade so you can make a decision that best serves you.

If you make a mistake, own it, take responsibility for it, apologize for it, forgive yourself, and move on, trying something different as you navigate toward your goal.

Tenacity happens when you keep moving on even though it's hard—even though the odds are stacked against you.

This life is your mission. Every day is an opportunity to make an impact—to do something that has never been done before.

CHAPTER 20

FEAR IS YOUR FRIEND

In order to fly the mission, I had to do the STABO mission. The "STA*bilized* BOdy" mission is an extraction method using a harness to rescue up to four soldiers from a field location where a helicopter cannot land.

It was a sunny, reasonably warm day for Fort Drum. Our company was gathered in a large training field with one helicopter, and instructor pilot Santos was certifying the pilots one at a time.

Being one of the "dopes on the rope" was not my first choice—or my second or my third! I wasn't afraid of heights—that wouldn't make much sense for a helicopter pilot—but I wasn't comfortable with hanging underneath a perfectly good helicopter I could be flying. I didn't have a choice though, if I wanted to perform the mission. I was committed to being out of my comfort zone and doing something different. But oh! I was scared, and I was nervous.

As I stepped into the thick, webbed belts of the harness that wrapped around every limb and my torso, time seemed to stand still. In between the pounding of my heart, I could hear every word

167

the field unit's sergeant running the groundside said. Every thud was loud in my ears, and I could see the Black Hawk make its way over the treetops to come around and release the first crew. As the helicopter slowly made its way back to the field area, it lowered closer to the ground slowly, slowly, just barely moving forward to let the lowest soldier step onto the ground and then the next, until all four were there.

The Black Hawk moved ahead, away from the troops who had unbuckled their harnesses. Then it landed, waiting for the next pilot change and four new "dopes."

I was up.

The two crew chiefs were lined up in front of me, and there was another pilot behind me. (Yes, I was the only female—again.)

"Ready?" the sergeant barked. It wasn't really a question. Our harnesses were checked. Then we double checked each other's and moved to the extraction area. In reality, it only took moments to hook up to the rope and be lifted into the air, but it seemed like an eternity of anticipation and heightened awareness.

I watched the legs and feet of the two crew chiefs above me. I was lifted one foot, then two, then five, and then there was a tug. The pilot below me was lifted off the ground too, his weight pulling on my ropes and harness. My harness became so tight it was difficult to breath. It pulled against my rib cage, and every heartbeat seemed slow. I saw the green trees, the sun sparkling on the babbling creek that wound through the trees, and as the helicopter started moving slowly forward, the summer air buffeted my face.

It. Was. Amazing.

I tilted my head back and laughed, and I saw the crew chief above me doing slow jumping jacks in the air and grinning. Below me, the pilot had his arms extended fully, hands open to catch the air. The rope swayed slightly as we turned back toward the training field. Our time was nearly done, and it felt as if we had just taken off. Yet every second of that exercise was imprinted indelibly into my memory.

Fear is not something to avoid. Fear is your friend. Fear is what tells you:

"You are ALIVE.
Pay attention;
this is important."

Living a life without fear means you are not trying anything different, not taking a risk, and simply living a life on autopilot. Use fear to heighten your awareness of what you should be paying attention to. Then step over that fear to get to what you want to achieve.

"Too many of us are not living our dreams because we
are living by our fears."
~Les Brown

We are all aware of how important it is to try something new, but many of us choose not to do so. This choice is often driven by our level of fear, the fear of change, of what people may say, or even of looking dumb. Those who rarely step out of their comfort zone often experience one or more of these fears. In order to break free of our comfort zone, we need to overcome our fears.

When we garner the strength we need to overcome these fears, we will soon realize that the world is a much larger place than we had first imagined.

Whether it is trying a new type of food for the first time or flying on an airplane, the decision to overcome your fear will lead to you living a more fulfilling and enjoyable life.

While it may be easier for some to accept these new experiences with open arms, there are plenty of people who simply can't take the leap. If you are one of these people, the first thing you should realize is that you are likely missing out on many different opportunities that could greatly improve your life and lead you to increased levels of success.

It all starts with a single step, and once you take that step, you will be surprised at how much easier it the next one becomes.

Facing your fear, embracing it, and stepping over it, leads to enlightened awareness. This is Tenacity. It's not giving up when you are afraid. It's being willing to go the extra mile when others would quit. It's pushing through the obstacles and trying something new, even though you might fail. It's learning from your mistakes and still being willing to try again from a different angle.

Your life is your mission. No one is responsible for you but you. This is your LIFE!

Believe in your **POTENTIAL** and be aware of what you can do.

Be willing to make decisions that support your potential and lead you to **IMPLEMENT** and take action.

Communicate, Aviate, and Navigate in everything you do, and with that, **LEADERSHIP** will rise within you.

Take care of yourself and **OPTIMIZE** your life, your actions, and your results.

When faced with adversity or fear, shore up your **TENACITY** and step outside of your comfort zone to lead yourself to greater achievements.

It's up to you to LEAD YOURSELF.

First Lead Yourself and FLY in your life.

CONTRIBUTING PILOT INDEX

Doug Petersen
Page 57

Doug Petersen is a retired U.S. Army aviator and Vietnam veteran. In Vietnam, he flew Dustoff helicopters. After his military career, Doug continued serving the military through a financial planning company. Today, he is an inspirational speaker and award-winning author.
www.inspirevalues.com

Kimberly Olson, Colonel, USAF (retired) Page 65

Kimberly Olson is the CEO/President of Grace After Fire, a nonprofit dedicated to helping women veterans. She joined the organization after twenty-five years of military service, including deploying to the combat zones of Bosnia and Iraq, serving at the Pentagon (surviving 9/11 attack), and becoming a command pilot with 3,700 flying hours in six different aircraft.
www.graceafterfire.org

Buck "Ballistic" Burney
Page 88

Ballistic has over 3,000 hours flying many of the nation's top fighters, including the F-16

and the F-15, for the Florida Air National Guard. Buck has an inspirational, motivational message for senior leadership as well as corporate employees on creating and maintaining synergistic high-performance cultures in organizations. www.missionontarget.com

Dan Bornarth
Page 94

Dan Bornarth is a career naval flight officer and radar intercept officer whose experience includes combat flights during Operation Desert Storm and a tour of duty as an adversary instructor in Key West, FL, with VF-45. After retirement, Dan formed the company HarborSite International, LLC, which specializes in security consulting, emergency response operations, and military and law enforcement training.
www.harborsite.net

Carol
Page 120

Commercial airline pilot
Full name withheld upon request

Tom Martinelli
Page 137

Tom Martinelli left the Army aviation after ten years of service and returned to graduate school to begin a second career as a health and safety professional. Tom is an avid photographer and lives with his wife in Atlanta, Georgia.

Dale Edelmann
Page 143
Dale Edelmann served in the U.S. Navy from 1993-1996, traveling all over the world. As a charter pilot, Dale specialized in professional aviation with over 4,400 hours flying King Air 350s, Piaggio Avanti's, and a Citation XLS. Dale's experiences as a pilot serve him well as a business owner and broker of Edelmann

The P.I.L.O.T. Method

Additional Titles from the Soar 2 Success Tip Series

Soar 2 Success in LinkedIn
Co-authored with Debbie Saviano

Soar 2 Success as You Create a Sales Roadmap
Co-authored with Debbie Mrazek

Soar 2 Success: Think Like a CEO
Co-authored with Alice Hinckley

Soar 2 Success with Coaching Skills
Co-authored with Dick Powell

Soar 2 Success in Marketing
Co-authored with Sandy Lawrence

Soar 2 Success in Real Estate Marketing
Co-authored with Tim Davis

Soar 2 Success with Email Marketing
Co-authored with Toni Harris

Soar 2 Success with Your Communication Skills
Co-authored with Kelley Moore

Soar 2 Success in Digital Strategy
Co-authored with AJ Amyx

Soar 2 Success with a Healthy Organizational Culture
Co-authored with Jim Gardner

Soar 2 Success with Your Customer Service
Co-authored with Anne Miner

And more books at Soar2SuccessBooks.com

The P.I.L.O.T. Method

Soar 2 Success
PUBLISHING

About Soar 2 Success International

Founded in 2012, Soar 2 Success International has rapidly grown to be a premier speaking and training company representing high-quality professional speakers.

Soar 2 Success added a publishing division in 2013 and already has more than twenty titles in process.

Find speakers, books, and publishing information at:

Soar2Success.com
Connect with us at:
facebook.com/Soar2Success
twitter.com/Soar2SuccessInt

179

The P.I.L.O.T. Method

ABOUT ELIZABETH

A sought-after international speaker, Elizabeth McCormick empowers audiences with her action-packed speaking. As seen on ABC News, "20/20," CBS News, MSNBC, FOX News Radio, and the front page of the Dallas Morning News, as well as in the Wall Street Journal, Elizabeth brings a unique and fresh perspective to everything she does.

As an Army Black Hawk helicopter pilot, Elizabeth flew missions such as Air Assault/Rappelling, Command & Control, VIP, and Military Intelligence. She also supported United Nations peacekeeping operations in Kosovo as the S-4 Logistics Officer in Charge at the battalion level, receiving the Meritorious Service Medal for her excellence in service. A decorated pilot and officer, Elizabeth was also awarded the Army Commendation Medal twice, the Army Achievement Medal three times, the National Defense Service Medal, the Humanitarian Service Medal, the Army Service Ribbon, and the coveted Army Aviator Badge.

She retired from the military as a Chief Warrant Officer 2, after a career-ending injury. Elizabeth was honored with the Congressional Veteran Commendation for her commitment to duty and community.

Elizabeth is a founding member of the John Maxwell Team of speakers, coaches, and trainers, as well as an award-

winning sales consultant who teaches sales training topics such as "It's Not Stalking; It's Follow-Up." A dynamic, energizing entertainer, Elizabeth inspires audiences with her pilot experiences and turns those stories into life or business lessons.

Elizabeth resides in the Dallas-Fort Worth Metroplex.

Book Elizabeth for your next event.
www.pilotspeaker.com

facebook.com/BlackHawkPilot
linkedin.com/in/BlackHawkPilot
twitter.com/PilotSpeaker
instagram.com/PilotSpeaker